"A book that is sure to stick, Wear Clean Underwear is part story, part education, and pure brilliance!"

—MICHAEL GERBER, FATHER, BESTSELLING AUTHOR OF *THE E-MYTH REVISITED* AND *AWAKENING THE ENTREPRENEUR WITHIN*, AND CHIEF DREAMER AT WWW.NEWDREAMINGROOM.COM

"I wish my family had read this book! Even though we employed the 'top experts' in estate planning, my mother was mired in the painful four-year probate of my father's estate after his death. This could have been avoided had we known what Ali shares in this book. EVERYONE needs to read it!"

—CHRISTINE COMAFORD-LYNCH, FORMER CEO AND FOUNDER OF MIGHTY VENTURES AND NEW YORK TIMES BESTSELLING AUTHOR OF *RULES FOR RENEGADES: HOW TO MAKE MORE MONEY, ROCK YOUR CAREER, AND REVEL IN YOUR INDIVIDUALITY*

"If you can't stand the thought of reading pages and pages of technical advice, but you desperately want to protect your child's future, this is the book for you."

—ABIGAIL DOTSON, HEALTHY HOUSE EXPERT AND MOM, WWW.HEARTHLA.COM

"If you want to leave your children financially and emotionally secure no matter what and never leave their welfare up to chance, Wear Clean Underwear is a must-read."

—MICHAEL PORT, BESTSELLING AUTHOR OF *BOOK YOURSELF SOLID* AND *BEYOND BOOKED SOLID*

"You know you should assign guardians. You know you should protect your assets. *Wear Clean Underwear* tells you the rest of the story."

"As parents, we spend so much time and effort on how to prepare our children for the future, yet we often overlook the reality of how to protect and secure our children's future if we're no longer around. Using compelling stories, Ali Katz reveals the critical steps parents must address to plan effectively for their children's future. An eye-opening and much-needed guide!"

"*Wear Clean Underwear* is an easy-to-understand guide for parents who want to leave their children not just with financial security but peace and guidance in case of any eventuality. By reading and applying the principles in the book, if the worst does happen, your family and friends will be left empowered instead of frustrated and confused. A must-read!"

"The strategies in Ali's book *Wear Clean Underwear* are essential reading for every parent. The wisdom in these pages has ensured the wellbeing of my entire family, especially my greatest source of joy: my daughter! Thank you for writing this much-needed book."

"*Do you wish you could stop worrying about your children's future so you could spend more time enjoying the present? Wear Clean Underwear provides the peace of mind of knowing your children will be safe and loved no matter where you are.*"

—ALLANA PRATT, MOTHER, NUMBER-ONE-RATED
RADIO HOST OF *HOW MAMA GOT HER GROOVE BACK*, AND FOUNDER OF ALLANAPRATT.COM

"*As a parent, you want to provide your children with love, support, and protection through every age and stage of their lives. Wear Clean Underwear is the perfect parent guide to provide you the tools, tips, and techniques to protect your most valuable asset— your family. And it does this in a fast, easy, and fun way!*"

—SANYIKA CALLOWAY BOYCE, FINANCIAL FITNESS COACH
AND AUTHOR OF *CRACK DA CODE* AND *TEEN MONEY TIPS*

"*A rare and devoted book that understands and integrates the multidimensional emotional, personal, and legal challenges of estate planning.*"

—RICHARD W. NEWMAN, PHD, FOUNDER
OF FINANCIALIFE PLANNING

"*Ali Katz is the authority on values-based estate planning for parents, and her book is about so much more than passing on financial assets: it's about love, values, family, and so much more.*"

—SUSAN WILSON SOLOVIC, FORMER CEO OF SMALL
BUSINESS TELEVISION (SBTV) AND AUTHOR OF *THE GIRLS' GUIDE TO BUILDING A MILLION-DOLLAR BUSINESS*

"*Wear Clean Underwear is a must-read for parents who want to ensure their children's safety and happiness.*"

—SHAY PAUSA, MOTHER AND FOUNDER
OF CHIKII WOMAN TO WOMAN

"Wear Clean Underwear will impact the way you think about your assets, values, and children. Now is the time to take action; it could save your children from paying excessive estate taxes or suffering a drawn-out probate. More importantly, what you do today could ensure your values are passed down for generations; leave the legacy you intended to leave. Read Wear Clean Underwear today and get started."

—LORAL LANGEMEIER, MOTHER, MASTER COACH, WEALTH STRATEGIST, BESTSELLING AUTHOR OF THE MILLIONAIRE MAKER BOOK SERIES: *THE MILLIONAIRE MAKER, THE MILLIONAIRE MAKER'S GUIDE TO WEALTH CYCLE INVESTING,* AND *THE MILLIONAIRE MAKER'S GUIDE TO CREATING A CASH MACHINE FOR LIFE,* AND FOUNDER AND CEO OF THE WEALTH-BUILDING COMMUNITY LIVEOUTLOUD.COM

"I constantly drill into my students the importance of having a competent, ethical, and honest Personal Family Lawyer. This is an attorney who is an expert in your state laws and willing to go the extra mile to get to know your family and special situation. Ali Katz is the personal family attorney who is taking this vital message to families nationwide. Her advice in this book is not just important, it's vital to the future of you and your children. I wish my father had read this book before his unexpected death and the resulting mess that was left behind, all of which could have been avoided had he known what Ali teaches you here."

—SCOTT BROWN, PHD, AUTHOR OF *THE WALLET DOCTOR'S SURVIVAL GUIDE TO THE STOCK MARKET*

"When it comes to the safety of your kids, what could happen after you are gone is as important as what happens during your lifetime: to know your kids would always be cared for by people you want in the way you want. Ali Katz tackles this subject with easy-to-understand, parent-friendly language and makes it simple for us to take action. Excellent—read this book!"

—PATTIE FITZGERALD, FOUNDER OF SAFELY EVER AFTER, INC., WWW.SAFELYEVERAFTER.COM

"*This book considers the complete realm of prosperity and wealth; it's not just money, it's what you do with your money and whether you use it to strengthen your values and provide a lasting legacy for your children.*"

—LORI MACKEY, FOUNDER OF PROSPERITY4KIDS, INC., AND AUTHOR OF *MONEY MAMA & THE THREE LITTLE PIGS*

"*To be a great parent today, you've got to think about your kids' futures after you are gone. Wear Clean Underwear makes it easy to do while giving you the tools you need to take the next steps.*"

—MARYANNE COMAROTO, MOTHER, AUTHOR OF *SKINNY, TAN, AND RICH: UNVEILING THE MYTH*, AND RELATIONSHIP ADVOCATE ON HEALTHYLIFE.NET

WEAR CLEAN UNDERWEAR

SECOND EDITION

WEAR CLEAN UNDERWEAR

A FAST, FUN, FRIENDLY—AND ESSENTIAL—GUIDE

TO LEGAL PLANNING FOR BUSY PARENTS

(BECAUSE *Wearing Clean Underwear* ISN'T ENOUGH)

ALI KATZ

LIONCREST
PUBLISHING

WEAR CLEAN UNDERWEAR
A Fast, Fun, Friendly—and Essential—Guide to Legal Planning for Busy Parents (Because Wearing Clean Underwear Isn't Enough)

SECOND EDITION

ISBN 978-1-5445-3588-3 *Paperback*
      978-1-5445-3589-0 *Ebook*

To Kaia and Noah, the loves of my life.

Without the two of you, I never would have embarked on this journey.

Thank you for sharing me.

CONTENTS

STORY THREE: YOU AND AIKO

A PERSONAL MESSAGE FROM ALI KATZ

The day my daughter was born, I became aware that a piece of me would live forever. It was no longer enough to wear clean underwear in case I ended up in the hospital; I needed to prepare for a whole host of other things, like who would take care of this little bundle of love that meant more to me than my own life if for some reason I couldn't do it myself. Suddenly, I was a mom. I was responsible for my daughter's life and keenly aware that my choices could ripple through future generations.

If you are anything like me, you do not want to think about dying. In the back of your mind, you secretly hope they find a cure for death before it is your time. But in truth, you have accepted that one day, you will die.

It is likely to be far in the future, when your kids are old and gray themselves, but no matter when it happens, you can use the knowledge learned by reading this book to focus on leaving the world a better place for your children and grandchildren.

Most of us have not planned at all for the time when we are no longer here. We plan for things that will likely never happen, like fires, hurricanes, and earthquakes. We plan for things that are not particularly important, like our trips to the grocery or hardware store. We spend an inordinate amount of time planning our children's birthday parties and playdates. So why do we fail to plan for things guaranteed to happen: our lives and eventual deaths?

Is it because we are too busy? Is it because we do not think we will die anytime soon? Or is it because we are scared?

Probably all of the above.

But as you will learn from this book, imagining what will happen if you do not plan is exponentially scarier. If you leave this Earth without specifically spelling out what you want to happen, the government will take matters into its own hands.

The government does not know your children. It does not know your spouse. And it wants as much of your money as possible.

In all truth, planning can be scary as well. Going to a lawyer's office and sorting through a whirlwind of legal terms like "probate," "per stirpes," "trustees," "executors," and "healthcare directives" is intimidating.

What if your lack of expertise leads you to the wrong choice?

If you only understood the legalese, the choices might be easier.

Wear Clean Underwear: A Fast, Fun, Friendly—and Essential— Guide to Legal Planning for Busy Parents not only boils down the complexities into simple, easy-to-understand terms but also guides you through unique stories that offer real examples of what would happen to your assets, children, spouse, or loved ones if you were in an accident based on the choices you make now. You will then have the context to make crucial decisions about your life and legacy.

In an easy-to-read story format, *Wear Clean Underwear* shows you how the preparations (or lack thereof) you make today will impact generations to come, guiding you quickly and easily to do the right thing for the people you love most.

This book is about living the best life you can, leaving the world a better place, and setting the foundation for the success of your spouse, children, and loved ones, no matter how long you live and no matter how much money you leave behind.

I've written three stories, each of which provides a layman's explanation of the legal issues surrounding planning for the care of your children and your money. "Story One: Sara and Carlos" is for those with minor children at home, whether you have significant resources or not. "Story Two: Chelsea and Alex" is for those who have resources and would like to provide guidance to their spouses and children about how to preserve those resources for generations to come. Finally, "Story Three: You and Aiko" is for those with adult children and maybe not a whole lot of assets.

At the end of the book, I've included additional websites with checklists and free resources detailing the avenues available to you in your own life and legacy planning journey.

Before we get started, let me explain a term you will see throughout this book: "Life and Legacy Planning."

* * *

While this is a book about estate planning, to me, "estate planning" has always seemed an old, outdated term that does not apply to the kind of planning you are thinking about as a parent. "Estate planning" suggests you are planning merely for the passage of your assets (your estate) after you are gone.

So, to better encompass all that actually goes into the type of planning we want to do, I've created a new name for what you are doing when you are planning for life and death as a parent. I call it "Life and Legacy Planning." And it is about so much more than passing on your assets.

Done right, Life and Legacy Planning prepares your children for a future without you, whether two weeks from now or fifty years from now. Life and Legacy Planning requires you to decide proactively how you want to leave the world, intentionally focusing on what you can do in the here and now to not only pass on your financial wealth but also your values, insights, stories, and experiences—also known as your "whole family wealth."

Life and Legacy Planning results in making confident legal and financial decisions throughout your lifetime so you can live your best life possible while you are here and create the best possible future for the people you love.

Legacy isn't just what happens after you die; it's created moment by moment as a result of each decision you make throughout your life.

Before we get started, here's a note about terminology and naming conventions. Each of these stories is written so you can step into the role of the narrator and put yourself in the shoes of the decision-making parent. To the best of my ability, I have kept all names gender neutral so the stories resonate regardless of whether you are a man, a woman, or non-binary and whether your parenting partner is a man, a woman, or non-binary.

In addition, for consistency and ease of reading, I have identified the person with whom you have children as your "spouse." If you are in an unmarried relationship, either by choice or because the law does not allow your marriage, please know I respect your circumstances, and you can substitute the word "partner," "ex-spouse," "life partner," "baby daddy," "baby mama," or whatever other term you use for the person you co-parent with where appropriate. (Some issues may differ depending on whether a couple is married or unmarried; I've included further information about that at the end of the book.)

Happy reading!

Ali Katz

story one

SARA AND CARLOS

YOUR YOUNG CHILDREN: THE LOVES OF YOUR LIFE

You and your spouse have created an amazing life together.

You love your son, Carlos, to distraction. He is kind, sensitive, helpful, and generous of spirit. He loves music, animals, and basketball. He warms your heart and makes you smile. You suspect he is a genius.

He cannot stand when you leave, not because he needs you, but because he loves helping you. When your daughter, Sara, was born, your love for Carlos grew exponentially. He calls Sara "his baby." He worries when she cries. "My baby is sad," he says, with tears in his eyes.

When pregnant with Sara, you and your spouse worried you would not love her as much as you love Carlos.

But your heart expanded to accommodate your love for Sara, and even though she is different from Carlos in just about every way, you love her just as much as you love Carlos.

Sara has a mischievous sense of humor and wreaks havoc everywhere she goes. She earned the nickname "Hurricane Sara" by the time she was two. She makes you laugh. You suspect she is a genius.

You and your spouse are kind, loving, and attentive parents who make a great effort to be actively involved in your children's lives. They are your primary focus. Your spouse, who works for a prominent marketing firm, tries not to work more than eight hours a day, though business sometimes requires an out-of-town trip.

You are fortunate enough to work from home. Because your children are your first priority, it is sometimes difficult for you to find time to work, especially with the constant interruptions.

To ease your burden a little, you and your spouse look for someone to help with childcare and household errands. Because the two of you are financially successful, you can afford to be picky. Eventually, after searching for months and interviewing countless people with whom you would never leave your children, you find the perfect nanny and assistant. Though she is only twenty, Courtney is mature beyond her years and has the patience of a grandmother. You hire her to run errands and care for Carlos and Sara when you need to meet with clients or face a looming deadline.

Courtney is wonderful. She plays games with your children, rarely loses her temper, and teaches Carlos and Sara to speak Spanish. Your children love her, and you trust her wholeheartedly.

One morning, you have a three-hour meeting with a client at his office. Your spouse is in France on business. On your way out the door, you remind Courtney to call your cell phone if she needs you, which you always leave on vibrate in case anything comes up.

When you arrive at the client's office, you learn your meeting has been postponed, though no one bothered to notify you. You are irritated, of course, but you decide to make the most of the time and grab a quick workout.

You park your car in the gym's vast parking lot and remember cell phones are not allowed inside. From the parking lot, you try to call Courtney, but you receive a busy signal. You wait a couple minutes and try calling again. The phone is still busy. This surprises you, and you make a mental note to have Courtney call the phone company to find out why the second line is not ringing.

You make a choice. Courtney is responsible and can handle anything in the unlikely event something unexpected happens while you spend an hour in the gym. You turn off your cell phone, stow it in your gym bag, and stash your bag in a locker. You tell yourself that after you warm up, you will sneak into the locker room and try to call Courtney again.

While jogging on the treadmill, you worry about the kids. You remind yourself to stop worrying. Courtney will be fine for a little while without you.

And then, the unexpected happens. An aneurysm in your brain that has lain dormant for years—unseen, hidden, waiting—explodes.

Later, the doctors explain the aneurysm had nothing to do with the fact that you were working out. It was just a time bomb in your brain that could not have been prevented, even with prior knowledge of its existence. It could have happened anywhere: at the grocery store, in line at the bank, at home with your kids.

But it happened while you were at the gym, with your gym membership, driver's license, and all other forms of identification in an anonymous locker; your cell phone turned off; and your car a needle in a haystack in the gym's parking lot.

The gym calls 911 immediately, but without any means of identifying you, no one knows to call Courtney. By the time the paramedics arrive, you are gone. You never have the chance to tell anyone about your kids or Courtney or that your spouse is on a business trip in a foreign country.

When you don't return home by 3:00 p.m., Courtney calls your cell phone, but the call is sent straight to voicemail. *The meeting must have gone long,* Courtney thinks. Still, she worries a little bit. It isn't like you to turn off your phone, and you always call when you are going to be late.

Things happen, Courtney thinks. *I'm sure everything is fine.* She tries to be positive.

Two hours later, she is panicked. She has been calling your cell phone every fifteen minutes. She calls your client, only to discover the meeting was canceled. She tries calling your spouse's cell phone, but the electronic voice says the phone is "out of the service area." Courtney starts calling your friends.

None of them have seen or heard from you. Courtney calls the local hospitals, but since she is not a relative, no one will give her any information.

Courtney tries to stay calm around Sara and Carlos. She feeds your children, and though she rarely lets them watch TV, she sends them to your bedroom to watch cartoons before making a phone call.

Does Courtney call the police, or does she call someone else?

If your babysitter calls the police, continue to the next section. If your babysitter calls someone else, skip to the section titled "Courtney Does Not Call the Police" on page 33.

COURTNEY CALLS THE POLICE

Because you and your spouse did not have any sort of plan in place for what Courtney should do if something like this happens, Courtney does not know she should wait to call the police until your children are safely in the hands of someone who has clear authority to stay with them in your absence.

When the police arrive, they question Courtney and ask if your family has any relatives in town. Courtney does not know of any. The police try locating an executive at your spouse's marketing firm, but by this time, the office is closed.

"We'll take over from here. You can go home," Officer Matzo finally tells Courtney, after questioning her.

"What will happen to Carlos and Sara?" Courtney asks.

Officer Matzo informs Courtney that Child Protective Services will be responsible for Carlos and Sara's care until the authorities locate you, your spouse, or another family member and run the necessary background checks.

Courtney volunteers to keep the children with her overnight, but the authorities do not know anything about her. Leaving Carlos and Sara with her without any legal documentation giving her the authority to care for them is a potential liability for the authorities.

"No, ma'am. You have got to go home now. The kids will be fine," Officer Matzo says in response to Courtney's continued pleading for him to allow the children to remain in her care.

Courtney refuses to leave until Child Protective Services arrives. She packs overnight bags for your children and promises them they will be back home the next morning. When the social worker from Child Protective Services arrives, four-year-old Sara begins sobbing. She clings to Courtney and refuses to let go. When the social worker tries to pry Sara's fingers away, Courtney and steady-tempered Carlos, now eleven years old, both begin crying.

"This is ridiculous!" Courtney tells Officer Matzo and the social worker. "The children want to stay with me, and I want them to stay with me. What is the problem?"

Officer Matzo explains that Courtney has no documented authority to stay with the children. Without such documentation, the police and Child Protective Services are legally responsible for the children. The officer and the social worker think Courtney is too young to care for young children overnight. And when the authorities run a background check on Courtney, they discover when she was seventeen and at a party following her high school graduation, she was arrested for possession of alcohol.

"You need to leave, ma'am," Officer Matzo tells Courtney forcefully. He says he needs to focus on your whereabouts, and Courtney's refusal to leave is slowing down the investigation. Giving your children a final embrace, Courtney has no choice but to leave. As she pulls away, she watches your children climb into the social worker's car.

Officer Matzo calls the local hospitals and is able to confirm your death. He alerts the social worker, who tells your children you are not coming home.

Because your spouse cannot be located, your children are put in the care of foster parents: Joe and Savannah Liardino. The Liardinos are kind, but they have four other foster children in their care, so they are not as attentive as they could be. Carlos and Sara are bewildered, terrified, heartbroken, and angry. Sara is too young to fully comprehend the situation and keeps asking about you. Carlos cries each time he tells his little sister you are not coming home.

"Why can't we stay with Gus and Patsy?" Sara asks Mrs. Liardino, referring to your dear friends and next-door neighbors Gustavo and Patricia Garcia. "We always spend the night with Gus and Patsy when Mommy and Daddy are gone." In fact, the Garcias think of your children as family and would have known how to care for them, but they did not answer the door hours earlier when Courtney knocked, looking for you. In the absence of any written instructions from you, neither the police nor the social worker tried to reach the Garcias.

The Liardinos know nothing about the Garcias. They do not know Patsy and Gus have two children who are friends of Carlos and Sara. They do not know your children often have slumber parties with the Garcias' children. They do not know Carlos and Sara love and trust Gus and Patsy and the Garcias would happily provide an immediate support system during a crisis.

The police do not know any of this because you never made a legal plan to tell them.

So instead of spending the first hours after your death embraced by a family they know and trust, your children are stuck with the Liardinos. The police are finally able to contact your spouse early the next morning, but bad weather delays flights out of Paris, and your spouse is unable to fly home for another forty-eight hours. In the meantime, your children become increasingly terrified and withdrawn. They think they may never see their remaining parent or home again and that they will be stuck with the Liardinos and their four foster brothers and sisters forever.

When your spouse finally arrives, Carlos is so angry he is having difficulty functioning; Sara is petrified to the point of catatonia. The oldest foster child in the home has been terrorizing Sara. Carlos has tried to defend her, but the older boy is bigger and stronger, and the Liardinos are indifferent.

Your spouse, who is equally devastated, takes your children home and tries to comfort them while dealing with the burden of notifying family and friends and arranging your funeral.

Your only living relative, your estranged brother, comes to the funeral with his wife. They sit alone, barely speak to your spouse, and leave without saying a word to your children.

After the funeral, your spouse enlists the help of a child therapist and calls on parishioners and clergymen for support. Eventually, your family begins to heal.

When Sara is seven and Carlos fourteen, your spouse begins dating again. You would have wanted this, but Carlos feels hurt and abandoned, as though your spouse is betraying your memory. Sara, on the other hand, is slowly forgetting about you. She was barely four when you died, so she has few memories of you.

Have you created a plan to make sure you remain a presence in your children's lives even after your death?

If so, turn to the section titled "You Left Written and Recorded Messages about Your Values, Insights, Stories, and Experiences for Your Children" on page 37. If not, turn to the section titled "You Did Not Leave Written and Recorded Messages for Your Children" on page 41.

COURTNEY DOES NOT CALL THE POLICE

You and your spouse have been thorough. When Carlos was born, you prepared a comprehensive Kids Protection Plan, which provides instructions to your children's babysitters, daycare providers, teachers, and school administrators detailing the people to call in the event of an emergency. By providing these instructions, Carlos and Sara's caretakers (including Courtney) know not to call the police until your children are safely in the hands of someone who has clear authority to care for them in your absence.

The first names on the list are your neighbors Gustavo and Patricia Garcia. Patsy and Gus have two children who are friends of Carlos and Sara. In fact, your children often have sleepovers with the Garcias' children, Travis and Sherry.

Although the Garcias are at the park, Courtney has their cell phone numbers, which you posted on the refrigerator when Courtney was hired. They return home as soon as Courtney calls them. The Garcias know your unexplained tardiness means something is wrong, and because you prepared, they know they need to take care of your children until you or your spouse is located.

Because you and your spouse were prepared, Patsy has a copy

of the document you signed giving her legal authority to care for your children temporarily in just this type of situation. With this in hand, she feels confident your kids will not be taken into foster care when the police arrive.

Together, Courtney and Patsy call the police. The police are relieved to learn the Garcias have documented legal authority to care for your children. Without such documentation, your children would most likely be taken into the custody of Child Protective Services and placed in a foster home until your spouse could be located.

During traumatic times, children are always better off with familiar family members or friends, rather than strangers, no matter how safe, friendly, or capable those strangers may be. Your forethought means your children will remain with people you know, love, and trust while the police track down your spouse and investigate your disappearance

Post instructions for your children's caregivers on your refrigerator and distribute copies to all daycare providers, babysitters, teachers, instructors, and school administrators. To create your own forms or find a lawyer to guide you through creating a Kids Protection Plan that includes all of these documents, go to KidsProtectionPlan.com.

The police call the local hospitals and discover you have died. They contact your spouse, but bad weather delays flights out of Paris for forty-eight hours. In the meantime, Patsy cares for your children. They are, of course, devastated and do not completely understand you will not be coming back. But because they love and trust Patsy and Gus, they have an immediate support system.

When your spouse arrives and takes your children home, they begin the process of grieving.

Your spouse arranges your funeral, calling on your friends for comfort. Your only living relative, your estranged brother, comes to the funeral with his wife. They sit alone, barely speak to your spouse, and leave without saying a word to your children.

After the funeral, your spouse enlists the help of a child therapist and calls on parishioners and clergymen for support. Eventually, your family begins to heal.

When Sara is seven and Carlos is fourteen, your spouse begins dating again. You would have wanted this, but Carlos feels hurt and abandoned, as though your spouse is betraying your memory. Sara, on the other hand, is slowly forgetting about you. She was barely four when you died, so she has few memories of you.

Have you created a plan to make sure you remain a presence in your children's lives even after your death?

If so, turn to the section titled "You Left Written and Recorded Messages about Your Values, Insights, Stories, and Experiences for Your Children" on page 37. If not, turn to the section titled "You Did Not Leave Written and Recorded Messages for Your Children" on page 41.

Carry a card in your wallet listing the names and contact information of the temporary guardians or first responders you have chosen to care for your children. Be sure you have given those people legal authority to take custody of your children in the event you are ill, become injured, or die, and give them instructions on what to do if something happens to you. Every Kids Protection Plan includes legal documents naming temporary guardians, an ID card for your wallet, and instructions to your babysitters for the fridge.

YOU LEFT WRITTEN AND RECORDED MESSAGES ABOUT YOUR VALUES, INSIGHTS, STORIES, AND EXPERIENCES FOR YOUR CHILDREN

The first time you felt Carlos kick, you thought about the life lessons you wanted to teach him: the values, insights, stories, and experiences you wanted to share with him when the time was right. You started a mental file of what you wanted him to learn; by the time Sara was born, that mental file was bulging.

The first time you spent a night away from Carlos and Sara, you realized all these life lessons were locked up in your mind, and if anything happened to you, Carlos and Sara would never benefit from your mental file. Your concerns resurfaced when Carlos was nine. You became aware of how many of his beliefs—beliefs you did not necessarily want him to have—were shaped by his schoolmates, TV, and teachers. You knew your chance to infuse his mind with life lessons was quickly passing.

You convinced your spouse to spend a weekend discussing the life lessons you wanted your kids to learn. Together, you wrote several letters and made recordings to be given to your children on specified birthdays, graduations, engagements, and on other milestone days, like their wedding days or when they each became parents themselves. You knew it was likely you would be reading the letters with them on those special days, but you felt peace knowing they would hear these life lessons from you even if you were not alive.

Though thinking about death is never pleasant, this weekend helped you and your spouse reach clarity on the values, insights, stories, and experiences you wanted to pass along. It also granted you the security of knowing you had a plan for passing on these values.

Both kids were growing so fast, and with a hectic day-to-day life, you realized how easily they could grow up without the benefit of all the important things locked in your head. Soon, they would be too wrapped up with friends to listen to your insights into life. After that weekend, you and your spouse were much more conscious about taking the time and creating the energy to share your values, insights, stories, and experiences at age-appropriate intervals.

As it turns out, you could not be at Sara's wedding. But after her soon-to-be husband proposes, Sara is given a letter from you about love and commitment. In the letter, you quote Kahlil Gibran's touching poem "On Marriage," writing, "...let there be spaces in your togetherness,/And let the winds of the heavens dance between you."

Sara incorporates this poem into her vows. She feels your spirit at her ceremony. And though she has few memories of you, she has been hearing your voice and reading your letters throughout her life. She knows you, and she feels your love.

Years earlier, when Carlos goes on his first date at the age of fourteen, your spouse gives him a letter from you. The letter speaks of the excitement of new romance and his responsibility to be an honest, thoughtful gentleman. That's when Carlos begins to realize you would have wanted your spouse to enjoy life with someone new and that he has been unfair. He finally recognizes your spouse should be able to enjoy the excitement without being blamed for betraying your memory.

Continue to the section titled "Your Spouse" on page 43.

YOU DID NOT LEAVE WRITTEN AND RECORDED MESSAGES FOR YOUR CHILDREN

The first time you felt Carlos kick, you thought about the life lessons you wanted to teach him: the values, insights, stories, and experiences you wanted to share with him when the time was right. You started a mental file of what you wanted him to learn; by the time Sara was born, that mental file was bulging.

Many times, you thought about spending a weekend with your spouse discussing the values, insights, stories, and experiences you want to share with your children, but life is so hectic you never scheduled time to create a plan to transfer your values to your children. You figure you will share the lessons when the time is right.

Your children are more important to you than your own life. They are constantly on your mind, so it never occurs to you *they* could forget *you*. Though your parents died when you were a young adult, you remember them with vivid detail.

Sara starts to forget about you within a few months of your death. Carlos will never forget you, but the older he gets, the less he feels he knows you and the more he feels is missing.

During milestone occasions, Carlos often wonders what you would have said. When your spouse begins dating, Carlos feels certain you would have disapproved (even though you wouldn't have). When he struggles with a difficult career choice—whether to follow his heart and be poor forever or follow the money—he wonders what you would have said (follow your heart). When his first child is born, he wonders what advice you would have shared with him (learn to laugh when the baby spits up on your new suit).

Continue to the section titled "Your Spouse" on page 43.

YOUR SPOUSE

Your family is doing as well as can be expected. The marketing firm that employs your spouse provided a yearlong sabbatical after your death, and fortunately, you had enough life insurance for your spouse to afford the time off. During this time, Sara starts afternoon kindergarten, and the family moves closer to the children's school. By the time your spouse goes back to work, both of your children are in school.

Since your death, your spouse has been in constant "drive" mode—driving your children to school, doctor's appointments, lessons, and all of the other activities the two of you wanted them to participate in. Courtney still helps around the house, but your spouse has double the responsibility and is chronically exhausted.

One day, while driving home from work with a friend in the car, your spouse falls asleep at the wheel. Awakened by a blaring horn and screeching tires, your spouse is alive for only a split second more before running into a semi-trailer truck. Your spouse's friend in the passenger seat also dies instantly.

When your spouse fails to pick up your children, Patsy and Gus know what to do. They locate the documents your spouse created after your death giving them the legal authority to serve as temporary guardians of your children, and they call the police.

Everyone is shocked to learn your spouse has died so soon after you. "What will happen to the children?" they ask.

Turn to the section titled "You and Your Spouse Named Guardians for Your Children" on page 45 if you named permanent guardians for your children. Turn to the section titled "You and Your Spouse Did Not Name Permanent Guardians for Your Children" on page 63 if you did not name permanent guardians for your children.

YOU AND YOUR SPOUSE NAMED GUARDIANS FOR YOUR CHILDREN

You considered what would happen if both you and your spouse died while your children were still minors. In fact, your parents were together when they died. Your father was an airline pilot who also had a private pilot's license. Though he was an expert flier, the single-engine plane he was piloting could not handle the storm that arose unexpectedly while he and your mother were making the short flight from Los Angeles to Santa Barbara.

Because you understood it was all too possible for children to lose both their parents, you insisted you and your spouse complete the paperwork to name permanent guardians.

If you had the guidance of a Personal Family Lawyer when preparing your guardian nomination, turn to the section titled "You Had Guidance from a Personal Family Lawyer When Preparing Your Guardian Nomination" on page 47. If you did not have the guidance of a Personal Family Lawyer when preparing your guardian nomination, turn to the section titled "You Did Not Have the Guidance of a Personal Family Lawyer When Preparing Your Guardian Nomination" on page 57.

YOU HAD GUIDANCE FROM A PERSONAL FAMILY LAWYER WHEN PREPARING YOUR GUARDIAN NOMINATION

The whole experience of naming guardians for your kids was much easier than you expected. You met with a Personal Family Lawyer named Mika, who not only prepared the legal documents for you but also counseled you to help you decide who should raise your kids, which was important to you because you and your spouse were not entirely sure whom to choose.

Other than your estranged brother, neither of you have any immediate family, and neither of you are close with your extended families. You were at a loss when it came to making a decision. Mika, your Personal Family Lawyer, helped you determine what was important to you when deciding who would raise your children. You knew you wanted your children raised by a married couple. You knew you wanted them raised in your own neighborhood. Additionally, because you and your spouse value cultural experiences, you wanted your children raised by guardians who value world travel and ideally speak more than one language.

You carefully considered couples who fit these criteria, share your spiritual values, and have similar parenting philosophies. Eventually, you decided on two couples you both considered the most likely to raise your children in an environment similar to the one you would have provided: Karl and Robin Couch and Patricia and Gustavo Garcia.

The Couches, both teachers, are less affluent than the Garcias. They certainly do not have enough money to send your children to private school, much less travel the world extensively. But they share your religion and parenting philosophy. In fact, you and your spouse have known Robin since college and always admired her values. Though you do not know Karl as well, you trust Robin would marry a man with similar convictions.

On the other hand, the Garcia children attend the same private school as your children, and they spend summer and Christmas vacations in South America. The whole family is trilingual. You and your spouse met Gus and Patsy years ago when you first moved into your neighborhood during college. Over the years, they became more than neighbors: they became your best friends. You love them both equally, and you trust them implicitly with your children.

Nevertheless, the values exercise you worked through with your Personal Family Lawyer helped you determine your religious values are most important to you. Because they share your religious values, you decided to make Robin and Karl your first choice as guardians. You figured with proper planning, you could leave behind enough money to have your children sent to private school and earmark funds for foreign travel.

Having trouble determining who would make a good guardian for your kids? Download the Choosing the Right Guardian worksheet at PersonalFamilyLawyer.com.

In case something happened to Karl and Robin, you listed the Garcias as your second choice as guardians.

Sadly, something *did* happen to Robin. The friend in your spouse's car, the passenger who also died instantly, was Robin.

Unless you had specified otherwise, Karl, a man you had only known a short time and who was only chosen as a guardian by virtue of your friendship with his deceased wife, would become the guardian of your children.

But fortunately, your Personal Family Lawyer, Mika, helped you see that because you had only known Karl a short time and wanted a married couple to raise your children, you should craft your guardian nomination so that the Couches would only take guardianship if they could act together. If they could not, you wanted your children to be raised by the next couple on your list: Patsy and Gus Garcia.

From there, your wishes became a bit confusing, but Mika helped you reach clarity. If Patsy and Gus could not serve together because something happened to one of them or they were divorced at the time of your death, you wanted Robin Couch to raise your children, even if she was divorced (or widowed), but only if she lived in California. If she did not live in

California, your next choice was Ann and Michael Cohen, who you knew would never leave California.

Here is what your guardian nomination looked like:

NOMINATION OF GUARDIAN

If a guardian of the person is required for any minor child of mine, I nominate Robin and Karl Couch jointly, so long as they are married and living together, to serve as guardians.

Alternate Guardians of the Person

If the above nominated guardians are unwilling or unable to serve or continue as guardians of the person of my minor child or children, then I nominate the following individuals to serve as guardians, listed in preferred order and not serving jointly unless so specifically noted:

Patricia and Gustavo Garcia, serving jointly, so long as they are married and living together in the State of California; then

Robin Couch, serving alone, so long as she is living in the State of California; then

Ann and Michael Cohen, serving jointly, so long as they are married and living together in the State of California; then

Patricia Garcia, serving alone, so long as she is living in the State of California; then

Gustavo Garcia, serving alone, so long as he is living in the State of California; then

Robin Couch, serving alone; then

Patricia Garcia, serving alone; then

Gustavo Garcia, serving alone; then

Michael Cohen, serving alone; then

Anne Cohen, serving alone.

This guardian nomination was then signed and witnessed by two independent witnesses over the age of eighteen and not related to you, in accordance with the legal requirements of your state for witnesses to a will.[1]

When you mentioned you never wanted your brother to take guardianship of your children under any circumstances, Mika prepared a confidential document to include in your plan that would stop your brother from assuming guardianship of your children.

The document would only be revealed if your brother and his wife tried to take custody of your kids. It states that in your opinion, your brother's wife is emotionally and verbally abusive to her own children. Your brother neglects his family, working sixteen-hour days so he can ignore the situation at home as his family spirals out of control. The confidential document clarifies that no matter how much they insist they have changed their lives, your brother and his wife are not to be named guardians of your children under any circumstances.

> Confidentially exclude those family members whom you would never want to take guardianship of your children. If these people challenge your choice of guardian, they will have little choice but to withdraw their challenge once the confidential document is revealed. Find a Personal Family Lawyer at PersonalFamilyLawyer.com if you have any complexities in your family dynamics, such as wanting to ensure a sibling or parent could never take custody of your children if something happens to you.

At the time of your spouse's car accident, your children are in the care of the Garcias, who call your Personal Family Lawyer.

---

1   Note: state law requirements for execution of a will vary, and you should consult with a lawyer in your state to review any legal documents you create for yourself.

Mika immediately locates your guardianship paperwork designating Robin and Karl Couch your first choice of guardians. Because Robin has died, your attorney arranges for your next choice, the Garcias, to assume permanent guardianship of Carlos and Sara.

In the meantime, your brother learns of your spouse's death. Upon hearing that your first choice of guardians, the Couches, are unable to serve, your brother and sister-in-law decide to challenge the Garcias' guardianship.

On paper, your brother and his family are picture-perfect. Your brother earns a large salary as the area's leading oncologist. They have a lovely home in a fantastic neighborhood. Your sister-in-law is a homemaker, an active member of the PTA, and a charming socialite who serves on the boards of several non-profit organizations and volunteers much of her time to charity work. The couple appears to value education, and their children attend only the best schools.

To prepare free legal documents and name guardians for your children, visit KidsProtectionPlan.com.

In the absence of any instruction from you and your spouse to the contrary, the court would no doubt give serious consideration to granting your brother and sister-in-law's request for guardianship. After all, the couple seems perfect, and the court would have no way of knowing about your sister-in-law's constant screaming or your brother's sixteen-hour work days. The court would not know that their own children's self-esteem has been so trampled by their parents' poor parenting skills and negative home environment that they have started to act out, choose the wrong friends, and make dangerous choices. The court would not know, for instance, that it would be sending Carlos and Sara to live in a home where the older children have already started to experiment with drugs and sexual activity.

But luckily, with the guidance of your Personal Family Lawyer, you thought ahead. And when Mika produces the confidential document excluding your brother and his wife, they immediately withdraw their petition for guardianship. They are hurt, ashamed, and angry. But they have no choice but to withdraw their petition for guardianship or suffer public embarrassment when your attorney and the courts are forced to expose the reasons for their exclusion.

Your children are protected, and, in accordance with your wishes, the Garcias become legal custodians of Carlos and Sara.

Patsy and Gus make exemplary parents. Gus is a musician, and he teaches Sara to play the guitar; he knows she wants to be a singer. He also notices Carlos' artistic gifts and enrolls your son in a weekend class for budding artists.

Patsy and Gus do everything you imagined they would. Because your Personal Family Lawyer impressed upon you the importance of leaving behind letters and recorded messages for your kids, Patsy and Gus have no confusion as to how you wanted your kids raised and the values, insights, stories, and experiences you wanted your children to have. They even raise them with the religious values that were so important to you.

Write letters to or record videos for your guardians with detailed instructions as to how you want them to handle such matters as religion and spirituality, education, career, money, values, and the like. Clearly indicate the people you want to be involved in your children's lives even in your absence. Every Life and Legacy Plan prepared by a Personal Family Lawyer includes encouraging you to record messages to your children and their guardians and create a Kids Protection Plan documenting who you would want raising your kids and being involved (or not involved) in their lives if you cannot be there.

When Sara tells the Garcias she wants to pursue her musical interests instead of attending a university, they smile and congratulate her because they know from your letters exactly how you wanted them to handle this situation.

"Not many people know what they want to do at such a young age," Patsy says.

"I know of a great community college you can attend part time. It has a phenomenal music department. You can take a general education course and a few music courses while still having time for music gigs," Gus says. "Can I set up an interview with the guidance counselor there for you?"

And Carlos? With the support of Patsy and Gus, Carlos's church (your church) introduces him to several international aid organizations. He is able to fight injustice by volunteering his time and efforts to developing countries.

In short, Carlos and Sara become people you would have been proud to call your children.

The last thing they do before going to bed each night is listen to the recording you made years before, when you met with your Personal Family Lawyer to plan for your life and your legacy, which Mika stored digitally. Sara and Carlos hear you and your spouse talk about the life lessons you hoped to pass on and the love you felt for them. Despite their grief at losing you, your children feel infinite peace and know everything will work out as it was supposed to, and they feel the loving embrace of an energy greater than themselves.

Congratulations. Your choice to plan for your life and legacy has the lasting impact of helping your children become their best selves and increasing your family wealth for generations to come. You have left the world a better place.

Continue reading Story Two on page 70 and Story Three on page 124 to learn more about Life and Legacy Planning, or turn to the Additional Resources section at the end of the book for more information about creating a legacy for your family.

YOU DID NOT HAVE THE GUIDANCE OF A PERSONAL FAMILY LAWYER WHEN PREPARING YOUR GUARDIAN NOMINATION

You figured it could not be that difficult to name guardians for your children. You went online to a legal-document service and downloaded the forms you needed.

But you were uncertain whom to name. Other than your estranged brother, neither you nor your spouse has any immediate family. Neither of you are close with your extended families. You were at a loss when it came to naming guardians.

One thing you knew for certain was you did not want your brother and his wife to take guardianship of your kids under any circumstances. From the outside, they look like a picture-perfect family, but your sister-in-law is emotionally and verbally abusive to her own children, screaming at them for the smallest infractions. Your brother ignores the situation. Instead, he works sixteen-hour days, neglecting his family as it spirals out of control.

You decided to name your closest friends Karl and Robin Couch or Patricia and Gustavo Garcia as guardians.

The Couches, both teachers, are less affluent than the Garcias. They certainly do not have enough money to send your children to private school, much less travel the world extensively. But they share your religion and parenting philosophy. In fact, you and your spouse have known Robin since college and always admired her values. Though you do not know Karl as well, you trust Robin would marry a man with similar convictions.

On the other hand, the Garcia children attend the same private school as your children. They spend summer and Christmas vacations in South America. The whole family is trilingual. You and your spouse met Gus and Patsy years ago when you first moved into your neighborhood during college. Over the years, they became more than neighbors: they became your best friends. You love them both equally and trust them implicitly with your children.

Nevertheless, because they share your religious values, you decided to make Robin and Karl your first choice as guardians. You figured with proper planning, you could leave behind enough money to have your children sent to private school and earmark funds for foreign travel.

When you and your spouse discussed potential guardians for your children, you both agreed that, if possible, you wanted a married couple to raise your children. Though you had known Karl for only a short time, you trusted Robin enough to know that she would marry a kind, decent man with strong values. The couple was newly married and head-over-heels in love.

They'll never divorce, you thought. But even if they did, you figured you would have enough time to update your guardianship paperwork to reflect that you would prefer Patsy and Gus Garcia to raise your children.

You never thought about what would happen if one of them died. You should have. You spend a lot of time with Robin, and you should have considered the possibility she might be with you if you die in an accident.

But you did not contemplate those things. Frankly, you just did not know about everything you should consider when creating these documents. Instead, you followed the online instructions, which did not suggest an individualized consultation with a lawyer trained to help you think through in-depth issues.

As luck would have it, you were not with Robin when you died, but Robin was in the car with your spouse at the time of their accident, leaving Karl as the guardian of your children.

This was not the worst-case scenario, but it was not ideal either. Karl and Robin married only a year before your death. Though you liked him, you did not know him well enough to entrust him with raising your children. And your children barely know Karl at all.

Karl is a good, responsible man. He cherishes his wife's memory, and as an extension of her, he loves all her friends. He wants to respect your wishes, so he agrees to serve as guardian of your children. After all, he has no evidence you wanted otherwise, and he assumes his religious affiliation guided your choice.

If you had worked with a Personal Family Lawyer, you would

have named Robin and Karl as your first choice but only if the couple remained married. You would have built in a provision to indicate that if the Couches divorced or either of them died, your children would be raised by Patsy and Gus Garcia.

When your spouse dies, your children are in the care of the Garcias, who locate the guardianship paperwork you have given them and call the police.

Karl is consumed with grief over Robin's death, but he feels a moral obligation to follow your apparent wishes to assume permanent guardianship, and he begins the guardianship process.

In the meantime, your brother learns of your spouse's death.

Your brother earns a large salary as the area's leading oncologist. His wife, your sister-in-law, is a homemaker. She is a member of the PTA. She is a charming socialite who serves on the boards of several nonprofits and volunteers her time to charities. The couple send their children to the best schools available. They live in a large home and seem to value education. From the outside, they are picture-perfect.

Except, of course, for your sister-in-law's constant tirades. And let's not forget your brother, who is a workaholic. Or their junior high school–aged children, who have had their self-esteem trampled for so many years they have already started to turn to marijuana and alcohol to self-medicate.

Upon learning of your spouse's death, your brother and sister-in-law immediately challenge the guardianship. Karl feels relieved. He is a man who would never shirk his obligation to care for Carlos and Sara, but he is overwhelmed. Karl does not know anything about your brother, but he hopes the courts grant your brother custody, and he withdraws his guardianship petition. He feels as if he's been let off the hook. *This is the perfect solution!* Karl thinks.

But when Gus and Patsy hear your brother has challenged the guardianship, they file for guardianship. Gus and Patsy know all the sordid details about your brother and his wife.

The ensuing custody battle is long and drawn out, with your children stuck right in the middle. Gus and Patsy, concerned for the wellbeing of your children, accuse your brother and sister-in-law of being terrible parents. Though Gus and Patsy's accusation is fair and necessary, you never would have wanted it made in a public forum. Embarrassed and hurt, your brother and sister-in-law dig up dirt on the Garcias.

What they find should be innocuous—in any other context, it would be meaningless and harmless. But in this situation, it is consequential. Your brother and sister-in-law discover that Gus was arrested for indecent exposure while in college. Of course, you already knew this because Gus moved into your neighborhood during college. In fact, you and your spouse were with him on the night in question, a night that involved too much beer and Gus's need to urinate right then and there—in public.

At the time, the event was embarrassing. In his adult years, it was fodder for jokes. One way or another, it was the innocent mistake of a young college student. Gus is an amazing father, a role model, and one of the best men you knew.

The courts don't know what to make of the situation. On the one hand, Gus and Patsy are high on your list of potential guardians. On the other hand, they are concerned with the best interests of your children, and your brother and sister-in-law appear perfect.

What do the courts decide?

Turn to the section titled "A Judge Chooses..." on page 67.

YOU AND YOUR SPOUSE DID NOT NAME PERMANENT GUARDIANS FOR YOUR CHILDREN

You considered what would happen if both you and your spouse died at the same time. In fact, your parents were together when they died. Your father was an airline pilot who also had a private pilot's license. Though he was an expert pilot, the single-engine plane he was flying could not handle the unexpected storm that arose while he and your mother were flying the short trip from Los Angeles to Santa Barbara.

The first time you and your spouse discussed naming a permanent guardian, you ended up in a fight. The second time, you were unable to choose between two couples.

Ultimately, you and your spouse wanted your children to be raised by people who live in your neighborhood, share your spiritual values, and have similar parenting philosophies. You considered which couples are well traveled, value foreign experiences, and speak several languages. This left only two couples: Patricia and Gustavo Garcia, and Robin and Karl Couch.

Though the Couches are less affluent than the Garcias, they share your religious values and parenting philosophy. The Garcias are the picture of culture. Their children know all about art and philosophy. They speak three languages and travel to South America for Christmas and France for summer vacations.

Both couples would have made excellent choices. You would have chosen Gus and Patsy. Your spouse was unsure but leaning toward the Couches.

Secretly, you told the Garcias you wanted them to be the guardians of your children. But you never documented anything. You considered making an appointment with a lawyer to help you reach a consensus, but you never got around to it.

You and your spouse did agree, in no uncertain terms, that you did not, under any circumstances, want your brother or sister-in-law to have custody of your children. Your sister-in-law is emotionally and verbally abusive to her own children. Your brother ignores the situation. Instead, he works sixteen-hour days, neglecting his family as it spirals out of control.

Had you made an appointment with a lawyer specifically trained to plan from a parent's perspective, you would have been advised to confidentially (but specifically) exclude your brother and sister-in-law from guardianship of your children in the event of your death or disability. The document would have specified that no matter what, your brother and sister-in-law would never be named guardian of your children under any circumstances. You would have created one, had you known.

It would have been a good idea.

As soon as your brother and sister-in-law learn of your spouse's death, they hire an attorney and petition the court for custody of Carlos and Sara. The Garcias, who know all of the sordid details about your brother and sister-in-law, also petition the court, requesting custody of your kids.

Your brother is the area's foremost oncologist, and your sister-in-law is a member of the PTA. She is charming and beautiful. She is married to a prominent doctor. She sends her children to the best private school available. She lives in a large house and values education.

On paper, your brother's family looks perfect. His large salary allows your sister-in-law to stay at home with the kids. The Garcias are a two-income family and both work full-time jobs.

The courts waste little time reviewing the two petitions. They never meet the Garcias or your brother and sister-in-law. They simply look at the petitions and make a decision.

What does the Judge decide?

Turn to the next section titled "A Judge Chooses..." on page 67.

YOU LEAVE BEHIND PLENTY, BUT HOW WILL YOUR CHILD AND SPOUSE HANDLE LIFE WITHOUT YOU?

You know all about wills, or at least, you think you do. When your grandmother died, she left you a bit of money, which meant you were suddenly in need of a will of your own. You turned to Mr. Thomas, the family attorney, who handled your grandparents' estate distribution and your parents' wills. Upon meeting with Mr. Thomas, you were impressed with his vast knowledge and ability to educate you. Mr. Thomas had been drafting wills for forty-five years, and you trusted him totally.

That was seven years ago. You have since married Alex, and together you have worked hard to increase your savings. You and Alex own a small home in Santa Monica, a real estate hotbed adjacent to Los Angeles, and when you add everything together, including your life insurance and the fair market value of your home, your children would receive an inheritance of almost $3 million if you both died.

You and Alex are planners. You plan to start a family in two years, once your careers are established, figuring you can both afford to take time away from work once you have a little more experience. Before your children are even conceived, you establish a $40,000 college savings plan for them with the money your grandmother left you. Of course, you and Alex each have a life insurance policy.

When baby Chelsea arrives, you feel the urgent need to update your will, which was drafted seven years ago, before Chelsea was born and before you were even married. You need to make sure you and Alex have wills that address your future as a couple, especially now that you have a child.

You want to schedule an appointment with Mr. Thomas, a seasoned veteran who has been loyal and trustworthy. Alex has read about lawyers who are specifically trained to plan for the needs of parents with young children, and Alex really wants to meet with a Personal Family Lawyer instead.

You suggest a compromise: "Let's make an appointment with both Mr. Thomas and a Personal Family Lawyer. We can make up our minds after we meet with both of them."

Mr. Thomas is near retirement and has a light client load, so he schedules your visit immediately. He is pleased to see you. You explain your situation, and Mr. Thomas agrees you should update your will and Alex should also have a will. He barely asks any questions before telling you he can send Alex's will and an updated copy of your will the following week. He suggests you leave everything to each other and then, upon the second spouse's death, to Chelsea.

Alex is skeptical. "He didn't ask any questions," Alex says. Still, Alex is impressed with the sense of urgency Mr. Thomas displays.

"Of course he didn't ask a lot of questions," you say. "He's been drafting wills for over fifty years. He could do this in his sleep."

Alex is convinced. "Let's cancel our meeting with the other lawyer," Alex says on the way home. "It all seems very boiler-plate. If I die, everything will go to you. If you die, everything will go to me. If we both die, it all goes to Chelsea, obviously. We don't need to visit another attorney to tell us that."

If you agree with Alex and decide to hire Mr. Thomas without meeting the other attorney, turn to the section titled "You Decide to Plan with Mr. Thomas" on page 75. Otherwise, turn to the section titled "You Keep Your Appointment with the Personal Family Lawyer" on page 77.

YOU DECIDE TO PLAN WITH MR. THOMAS

You and Alex agree that Mr. Thomas's more than fifty years of experience trump anything the Personal Family Lawyer might have said, and you call Mr. Thomas immediately to tell him your decision. Mr. Thomas says he will mail your wills the following week.

Your wills arrive on schedule. The documents look standard. If you die, everything goes to Alex. If Alex dies, everything goes to you. If you both die, everything goes to Chelsea. Alex's sister Kaari, who lives in the same city, is named Chelsea's guardian. In case Kaari is unable to assume guardianship, Alex's parents are your backup choice. You name your parents executors of your will and guardians of the estate; if they die, Kaari is the backup choice.

Speaking of your new daughter, Chelsea is a handful! As a result, you and Alex both take eight-week leaves of absence from work to care for her. Unfortunately, when you return to work, your company immediately sends you on an emergency out-of-town trip. You are heartbroken to leave Chelsea and Alex, and your company promises not to send you on any more trips for at least six months.

You are sent to a small, quaint town in Northern California. Because this is a last-minute trip, you are unable to find a hotel room and instead are one of three guests at the local bed and breakfast.

The same day you arrive, a contractor running an electricity conduit under a road inadvertently pierces a propane line. Unbeknownst to anyone, the propane settles directly underneath the bed and breakfast. While you are sleeping, the propane explodes, killing you, the owners of the bed and breakfast, and two other guests.

With a two-month-old baby to care for, Alex has no time to grieve. Your assets, which you and Alex held jointly, are transferred to Alex directly with no estate tax and no court involvement. The $1 million of life insurance is deposited into Alex's bank account.

Does Alex remarry? If so, turn to the section titled "Alex Remarries with the Wills Provided by Mr. Thomas" on page 93. If not, turn to the section titled "Alex Does Not Remarry with the Wills Provided by Mr. Thomas" on page 97.

YOU KEEP YOUR APPOINTMENT WITH THE PERSONAL FAMILY LAWYER

Despite your comfort level with Mr. Thomas, Alex's initial resistance has rubbed off on you. "There's no harm in seeking a second opinion," you tell Alex.

Together, you and Alex find a Personal Family Lawyer by visiting PersonalFamilyLawyer.com. Natalie ("Nat") Henson's office is just moments from your home. When you call to make an appointment, you can already tell the visit with Nat is going to be an entirely different experience from your meeting with Mr. Thomas. Nat's scheduling assistant, Susan, explains that Nat only takes on a few new clients a month because her process is not a one-size-fits-all plan for everyone. Instead, Nat follows a Life and Legacy Planning process of discovery that allows her to truly get to know you, your assets, and your family dynamics so she can help you choose the right plan for your family at the right budget.

Susan mentions that the Life and Legacy Planning process with Nat is normally $750, but if you are willing to do a little homework ahead of time, she can waive the fee for you. She asks if you'd like to hear the details. Mr. Thomas was only going to charge $2,000 total for all your estate planning documents, so $750 sounds like a lot, but you tell Susan you would like to hear more.

Susan explains that most estate plans are made up of the same basic documents, just like what Mr. Thomas was going to provide—a will, a healthcare directive, power of attorney, maybe a trust, and guardian nominations for Chelsea. "But," Susan says, "these documents can now be done online for free. What *really* matters is what happens during the process of creating the documents and after the documents are created."

Susan goes on to tell you that with the traditional process, like what you experienced with Mr. Thomas, most lawyers don't understand how to take into account the unique complexities of each family's situation, so the lawyer often makes decisions for you without really helping you understand the impact of those decisions.

This was exactly what you felt when you met with Mr. Thomas. You didn't understand what all the options were, so you were relying on Mr. Thomas's years of experience to tell you what to do, but you didn't really comprehend any of it.

Then, Susan explains, after the documents are created, they end up sitting on a shelf or in a drawer, an expensive stack of paper that isn't really what your family needs when something happens to you. Your family doesn't know what you have, how to find your assets, or whom to call.

And, because Mr. Thomas likely won't stay in touch with you at all after he delivers your documents, your documents may be so old by the time you become incapacitated or die that you find they are no longer even relevant. Everything in your life may have changed, your assets may have changed, and the law may have changed many times over.

You find yourself nodding, as Susan is speaking to the exact thing you were worried about when you met with Mr. Thomas, but you couldn't quite put it into words. While your family situation is very simple in some respects, you also know there are complexities that Mr. Thomas didn't bring up but you know would likely become a problem if something happens to you.

You also find yourself remembering that Mr. Thomas didn't ask about your new business or the business bank accounts you have. Similarly, he didn't ask about your cryptocurrency accounts, which no one would be able to access without you.

And while it seems obvious Alex's sister would take Chelsea if anything happened to you and Alex, you aren't so sure Kaari is the right person to take care of the finances for Chelsea.

You start to realize maybe there is more to these decisions than you originally thought.

Susan tells you that the Life and Legacy Planning process begins with a Family Wealth Planning Session, a two-hour working meeting where you'll review your assets and family dynamics with Nat. Nat will then teach you about the law and how it will apply to you, Chelsea, and Alex if something happens to you.

She explains that during this Family Wealth Planning Session, Nat will go over what would happen under the State's plan for you and help you understand what you might want to be different than what the law would provide if you did nothing. Susan again states that because this is a working session, it's two hours long and costs $750, but if you are willing to do some homework ahead of time—watch a webinar to get a little more educated in advance and submit some homework that will help your family no matter what if something happens to you—Susan can waive the Family Wealth Planning Session fee.

You have to wait several weeks for an appointment with Nat, but Susan assures you she will send a pre-meeting package so you can begin to prepare for the meeting.

The preparation package you receive before the meeting asks all sorts of questions about your family, values, and assets. As you complete the worksheets, you are surprised to find just how much you have to pass along.

You start thinking about answers to questions like these:

- Who would raise Chelsea if you could not? Is Alex's sister really the best choice, or should you consider close friends who share your parenting values?
- Who will guard the money you leave behind for Chelsea?
- Do you want Chelsea to receive her inheritance outright, or would you prefer she receive it at an age-appropriate time designated by you? Or, even better, in a lifetime asset protected trust she can control when she is old enough but will be safe from a future divorce or lawsuits?
- If you die first, do you want Alex to be able to leave the money you acquired together to a future spouse?

You had no idea there was so much to think about. Mr. Thomas did not mention any of this during your brief meeting.

When you arrive for your appointment, Nat greets you with a smile. Nat is quite a bit younger than Mr. Thomas, and she begins by telling you how her law firm works and what makes her practice different from the traditional and, in her opinion, antiquated practice of estate planning.

Nat describes the typical estate planning experience. It sounds just like the experience you had with Mr. Thomas!

Nat explains that in the traditional experience, clients meet with a lawyer who prepares form documents that the clients sign without really understanding all of their options completely. The clients then take those documents home, mark "Estate Planning" off their checklists, put the documents in a drawer or on a shelf, and never look at them again.

"The unfortunate part," Nat says, "is the planning documents are stale almost as soon as the clients leave the office. On top of the fact that the client never really understood the documents, their lives change, their assets change, and even the law changes, but those documents just stay the same."

And even though people know things have changed, they are reluctant to call their lawyers because they know they will be billed hourly in six-minute increments for each call. Nat tells you she billed $400 per hour when she worked at a big, traditional law firm!

Nat then goes on to explain that when clients called her old law firm, she was often unable to respond to even quick questions for hours or days at a time because she did not have a support team; she was the only person responsible for taking care of all the planning details.

As a result, she saw a lot of plans fail when families needed them most and when it was too late: after death or incapacity. Assets were owned incorrectly, documents were outdated, and family members did not know what to do or where to turn during an already emotionally difficult time.

Nat says she went to law school to make a difference in people's lives, be a lifetime advisor, and then be there for a client's family when the client cannot. Until she became a Personal Family Lawyer, Nat was seriously disappointed with her career choice.

Nat explains that working with a Personal Family Lawyer is a totally different experience. First of all, Personal Family Lawyers do not charge hourly fees, which means you can call anytime without receiving a bill in the mail a couple weeks later.

She talks about her team, which is available during office hours to answer quick questions and around the clock to address emergencies. If you need to talk with her about something more strategic or legal in nature, Nat assures you she will be available for a scheduled call, so you will never have to leave dozens of messages and go back and forth playing phone tag.

Then Nat tells you your plan is certain to work over time—even as your life changes, the law changes, and your assets change— because her office has systems in place to ensure you review and update your plan regularly.

Best of all, Nat talks about helping you pass on more than just your financial wealth to Chelsea. She introduces the concept of "whole family wealth," explaining that financial wealth is just a small part of a person's wealth. The most important parts of family wealth are actually intangible assets, such as intellectual, spiritual, and human assets or values, insights, stories, and experiences.

Nat tells you these intangible assets are most often lost when someone dies. "Think about your own grandparents or great-grandparents," Nat says. "What do you know about them?"

You realize you know very little about your parents' grandparents. Indeed, you do not even know their first names. Your grandmother left you a nice financial inheritance, but none of her childhood stories or experiences were captured—and you can't remember her voice at all.

Your grandmother might have passed on her values to you, for better or worse, but which of these values will you consciously pass on to your children in honor of your grandparents? And which ones do you want to leave behind forever?

It dawns on you that Chelsea will never hear your grandma's voice telling her how much she loves her. And it bothers you that if the tradition continues, Chelsea's grandchildren will not even know your name.

Nat says she uses a tool called a Family Wealth Legacy Interview, which is designed to capture and pass on these intangible assets. It all feels so much more personalized, which comforts you as you consider Chelsea's future.

Nat explains that the first step is to discuss exactly what would happen to Chelsea and your money as things currently stand. If you are unhappy with the status quo, Nat tells you she can help create a plan to make sure your daughter, assets, values, and legacy are protected in the event of your death or incapacity.

You are shocked when Nat tells you what would happen if you left your future in the hands of a will.

It turns out that because your parents and Alex's parents live all across the United States, Chelsea could actually be taken into the care of Child Protective Services temporarily if anything happens to both you and Alex!

Mr. Thomas did not mention anything about this.

As you discuss this scenario with Nat, you can see how obvious it is. If anything happened to you, your wills would be at Mr. Thomas's office, and no one would even know where to find them. Your parents would be hours away, and the authorities would not have any instructions on how you want Chelsea cared for in the meantime.

Of course, the police would call in Child Protective Services, and they would have no choice but to take Chelsea from your home. You are shocked Mr. Thomas failed to tell you this critical information!

You are even more shocked when Nat shows you how ill protected your money is with just wills.

Your house and bank accounts, as well as most of your holdings (except life insurance and certain retirement accounts), would have to go through a long and expensive court process called "probate." This means the money you left behind would be tied up in court for twelve to eighteen months, minimum.[2] And the court process could cost your family as much as $150,000,[3] with much of that going to Mr. Thomas!

THE TRUE COSTS OF PROBATE

Probate is, in essence, a lawsuit filed against your assets for the benefit of your creditors. During the probate process, the courts determine exactly how much of your assets should be divided among your creditors and how much should go to your family.

In California, for example, the cost of this court process can be as high as 5 percent of your total assets—even if you don't have any creditors. Aggravating matters, that 5 percent is calculated on the sale value of your assets, not counting any liabilities or debts against your estate. So, you could have a house worth $1,000,000 with an $800,000 mortgage (and just $200,000 of equity), and the entire probate cost would be calculated based on the $1,000,000 house value, not the $200,000 of equity.

But the costs of probate are not limited to the financial. There is also a time cost, as the probate process can take anywhere from a few months to more than a year (and can be even longer)—during which time your beneficiaries will not have free access to, or the use of, your assets.

Consider also the emotional cost your family pays by having this process dragged out for months or years, forcing them to undergo the arduous court process and preventing them from finding closure after their loss.

Finally, your loved ones pay a loss of privacy. Because probate rulings are public record, anyone can see who your beneficiaries are, how much they receive, and when they receive your assets. This leaves them open to unscrupulous predators who specifically look for people receiving large inheritances.

Ultimately, it is your family who is left with all these costs after you are gone. Is it worth it? (If not, visit PersonalFamilyLawyer.com to find a lawyer who can help you choose a better way to protect your assets *and* your loved ones.)

---

2   Per the California probate system. Each state has its own probate process, some of which are more onerous than others. Consult a Personal Family Lawyer in your state for specifics about what will happen if your assets go through probate.

3   In California, the cost of probate is approximately 5 percent of your total gross estate (meaning the total fair market value of your assets). To calculate the cost of probate for your family, contact a Personal Family Lawyer in your state.

You are blown away to discover that when both you and Alex die, your estate may have to pay estate taxes. You and Alex do not feel like rich people, but because of your life insurance and home, it turns out you already have nearly $3 million in assets—and while that's not currently subject to estate taxes, it potentially could be in the future.[4]

If you die and Alex lives, the wills offer no protection at all against future spouses, which means Alex can remarry and give all your assets to a new spouse. And worst of all, if both you and Alex die, Chelsea could inherit everything outright and totally unprotected when she turns eighteen.

Nat asks you and Alex to each share the one thing you wish you could change about the current plan.

It is hard for you to know where to start.

You and Alex agree that guardianship issues are your highest concerns. With respect to finances, you are most concerned with the probate process. Though you are not particularly concerned about the cost of probate, you do not want to put your family through twelve to eighteen months of courts and lawyers. You want to make it as easy as possible for them if anything happens to you.

Alex, on the other hand, is particularly concerned about estate

---

4   In 2008, when this book was first written, any estate in excess of $2 million was subject to the federal estate tax. Currently, in 2022, the federal estate tax only applies to estates over $11.5 million, but states like Minnesota, Oregon, and Massachusetts tax estates as small as $1 million. (As of this writing, Nebraska taxes inheritances over as little as $10,000!) And, the estate tax changes with each election, so contact your local Personal Family Lawyer for a complete analysis of the costs of probate plus estate taxes in your state and county.

taxes. If the estate tax exemption amount drops back to where it was in 2007 ($2,000,000) or even 2017 ($5,490,000), and your assets grow, that could mean that 45 percent—or $450,000 of every $1 million in assets—would go straight to the government.

"The good news," says Nat, "is that we can make sure there is no court process at all and no estate taxes. The only people who have to deal with probate and estate taxes are family members of people who do not plan or plan improperly.

"All we have to do is properly inventory your assets using our Personal Resource Map and Family Wealth Inventory and then take your house and bank accounts and put them into a revocable living trust. We then name the trust as the beneficiary of your life insurance policies and the second beneficiary of your retirement accounts. Your spouse will remain the first beneficiary. And, of course, we need to keep that inventory of your assets updated throughout your lifetime because we know things will change as the years go by."

"Once we do that," Nat tells you, "when something happens to you, your family will know what you have and where it is. Instead of having to deal with a court to get access to your assets, your family will come here to meet with me, and I can handle everything. Chelsea or her guardian could *immediately* access your assets per the terms you specify."

Nat turns to Alex. "And the assets would be free of any and all estate taxes so long as your assets stay below two times the exemption amount. And if they don't, because the exemption goes down or your assets go up, we'll be in contact and can update your plan to account for changes. We can even protect

Chelsea's inheritance so it is never at risk if she gets divorced or a lawsuit is filed against her when she is an adult."

"That sounds great," says Alex. "But I'm not entirely sure I understand what a trust really is."

Nat explains that a trust is an agreement between the person who has assets to put into the trust (also called the grantor, trustor, trustmaker, or settlor) and the trustee, who agrees to hold those assets for the benefit of the beneficiary.

"There are three important roles in a trust agreement: the *grantor*, who gives assets to the *trustee*, who holds them for the benefit of the *beneficiary*. The trust agreement is basically just a set of instructions telling the trustee how you want everything handled.

"While you are both living, you are in all three of those important roles. You are the grantor, the trustee, and the beneficiary, so you have not given anything up by putting your assets into the trust.

"Think of a trust as a treasure chest in which you store all your assets, including your home, your investments, your savings accounts, and everything else you own," Nat continues. "Once you put your assets in the treasure chest, you do not own them—your treasure chest does. But, as long as the trust is revocable—which is what we're creating for you today—you can open that treasure chest anytime you want. You have full control of everything in the treasure chest."

"This sounds too good to be true," you say. "Are there any downsides?"

"Here's the amazing part," says Nat. "There is no downside to having your assets inventoried and put into a trust. Sure, it will cost you some money now—approximately $4,000 to $6,000[5]— to get it set up, but the cost is far less than the cost of probate, estate taxes, and the nightmare your family will face if something happens to you without a plan in place.

"Plus, we aren't just preparing a trust for you. We're creating a whole Life and Legacy Plan, which is the beginning of a lifetime relationship with our law firm, so you and your family will have somewhere to turn throughout your life. And the best part is we will be here for your family when you cannot.

"And if you move to another state or something happens to me, you do not have to worry because we have our own Life and Legacy Plan in place, and you will be well taken care of by our designated Personal Family Lawyer in our state, or you can transfer your plan to a Personal Family Lawyer in any state you may move to in the future.[6]

"The most important thing you need to know when establishing a Life and Legacy Plan is that as your life changes, as your assets change, and as the laws change, your plan needs to change too. That means we'll stay in contact with you to keep you informed about legal changes—but you also need to keep in touch with

---

5   This approximation varies by lawyer and by state. Be wary of attorneys whose fees are significantly less than this, as a sharply reduced rate likely indicates you are merely buying documents instead of hiring a lawyer who focuses on guiding you through a lifetime of the right legal and financial decisions and will be there for your family when you cannot. In that case, your estate plan is likely to fail when your family most needs it.

6   Note that there are additional fees associated with transferring your plan to a Personal Family Lawyer in another state, as your plan will need to be updated to comply with your new state's laws.

us about changes in your life or assets so we can ensure your plan and ownership of your assets stay up to date.

"You don't have to worry too much about it now. We will guide you through the whole process. And we'll make sure your plan continues to work throughout your lifetime by reviewing it regularly. No doubt your life, your assets, and the law will change many, many times before your death, and we want to maintain your Life and Legacy Plan accordingly.

"If all that sounds good, we can go through a series of questions that will allow me to design the best possible plan for you and your family."

You and Alex do not even need to discuss it; the choice is obvious. "I'm sold," you say to Alex, who nods enthusiastically in agreement. "This is our Personal Family Lawyer."

You turn back to Nat and say, "Let's get started."

Over the next forty-five minutes, you answer questions you never had thought about before. When you leave, you feel a tremendous peace and calm, knowing everything will be taken care of if anything happens to you.

You call Mr. Thomas and tell him you have decided to go with another attorney. You feel slightly guilty, so you thank him for all the work he has done for your family and ask if you can take him to lunch.

Over lunch, you explain your decision. Mr. Thomas understands and admits he really doesn't have the systems and processes in his office to make planning with him much different than what you could do yourself online for free. He is retiring the following month and calls himself an "old-fashioned attorney." You feel less guilty when Mr. Thomas says, "You sound like you are in good hands. I won't have to worry about you when I retire." Mr. Thomas asks to see a picture of Chelsea, who is almost five weeks old.

"She is a delight, but Alex and I have our hands full!" you say.

In the coming weeks, your new attorney sends you a confirmation of all the important decisions you made and an inventory of your assets to confirm you haven't overlooked anything. Nat begins to prepare your Life and Legacy Plan.

Once you sign your documents, she guides you and Alex through the transfer of your assets into the name of your trust, all while you and Alex are out on parenting leave. She helps you create a set of guidelines for your guardians and trustees about how you want Chelsea to be cared for if you cannot be there. Nat also connects you with an insurance advisor, who helps you get more insurance protection in place, and a financial advisor, who helps you properly change the beneficiaries on your retirement accounts.

Unfortunately, as soon as your leave ends, your company immediately sends you on an emergency out-of-town trip. You are heartbroken to leave Chelsea and Alex so soon, and your company promises not to send you on any more trips for at least six months.

You are sent to a small, quaint town in Northern California.

Because this is a last-minute trip, you are unable to find a hotel room.

Instead, you are one of three guests at the local bed and breakfast.

The same day you arrive, a contractor running an electricity conduit under a road inadvertently pierces a propane line. Unbeknownst to anyone, the propane settles directly underneath the bed and breakfast. While you are sleeping, the propane explodes, killing you, the owners of the bed and breakfast, and two other guests.

With a two-month-old baby to care for, Alex has little time to grieve. Alex calls Nat, and together they move the assets as directed by the trust. Your $1 million life insurance policy is put into a special trust that Alex controls and can use but cannot give away to anyone other than Chelsea. The trust also provides that its assets cannot be taken from Alex in the event of a lawsuit. Pursuant to Nat's advice, Alex puts half of the assets you acquired together during your marriage into this second protected trust as well.

Does Alex remarry? If so, turn to the section titled "Alex Remarries with a Trust" on page 107. If not, turn to the section titled "Alex Does Not Remarry with a Trust" on page 115.

ALEX REMARRIES WITH THE WILLS PROVIDED BY MR. THOMAS

Heartbroken, Alex spends several years trying to move forward and finds comfort only in work and your daughter, Chelsea. Alex works day and night and begins investing in cryptocurrency, turning the $3 million you built together into $10 million. Doctors and friends tell Alex to slow down, but work helps ease the pain of your death.

Luckily, Alex meets JJ, a co-worker and fellow work-first go-getter. JJ has sole custody of two children and a mountain of debt from a previous marriage. Eventually, JJ and Alex marry and do what most couples do: combine their assets. They have joint bank accounts, their home is owned in both JJ and Alex's names, credit card accounts are held jointly, and Alex pays off JJ's debt.

Although both JJ and Alex work too much, Chelsea and her two step-siblings are relatively happy and well-adjusted children. Alex and JJ are both good providers who want the best for all three children.

Alex and JJ are so focused on their careers, though, that they are somewhat neglectful and indifferent when it comes to providing emotional support and involvement. But the three step-siblings are close. And because Alex and JJ are so well off, the children are able to participate in many school activities and find support in extended networks of school friends, parents, coaches, teachers, and the like.

In what seems like the blink of an eye, sixteen years pass from the time of your death.

Then, at the young age of fifty, Alex dies. For those who knew Alex, this was not a big surprise. Alex was bound to have a heart attack, given the stress and fatigue associated with consistently working sixteen-hour days. In fact, since your death sixteen years prior, Alex had not taken more than a few days of vacation. Upon Alex's death, Alex's $10 million estate (which includes the assets you left when you died) goes directly to JJ, as Alex's surviving spouse. Unfortunately, half of that was held in crypto-currency accounts that are lost when Alex dies because JJ has no idea how to access them, and Alex didn't leave clear instructions.

When you buy cryptocurrency, your account or wallet can only be accessed by private keys. If those private keys are lost, your account is essentially gone. Nobody has access to it.

With some crypto exchanges, such as Coinbase, the person named or appointed as the executor of your estate can show that paperwork to Coinbase and get access to the account, but only after going through the court process called "probate," which can take several months, or even years, and be quite expensive.

To ensure your cryptocurrency assets are not lost, discuss your holdings with your Personal Family Lawyer and confirm your lawyer has included planning for the immediate transfer of and access to these assets upon your incapacity or death without court intervention.

Nothing goes to Chelsea.

Chelsea suffers tremendously over the loss of Alex. Luckily, she has loving step-siblings and a staunch support network through school and all of her extracurricular activities. She is also lucky because JJ thinks of Chelsea as her own child and does not think twice about supporting Chelsea in the same way Alex would have, and there's still plenty of money, even with the lost cryptocurrency.

When Chelsea graduates from high school, she is able to attend the university of her choice. She maintained high grades throughout high school and had numerous sporting and other extracurricular activities on her résumé. Between the grants and scholarships she receives and JJ's assets (which are primarily the assets you and Alex earned that Alex grew), there are no limits on the amount Chelsea can spend pursuing higher education. She excels in the sciences, intends to attend graduate school, and ultimately wants a job in the field of biotechnology. Through your hard work, and that of Alex and JJ, Chelsea has everything going for her.

But then, during Chelsea's sophomore year of college, JJ dies while driving home late from having cocktails with an important client.

Although unfailingly committed to Chelsea in life, Alex and JJ had not made plans to ensure an equitable distribution of assets upon their deaths.

JJ's will was signed before even meeting Alex. JJ had always meant to get around to updating it but never did. At JJ's death, the estate goes through a long, costly probate. Because nothing was ever put in trust after Alex's death, neither Chelsea nor her step-siblings have access to the funds during the probate process.

When all is said and done, between probate and the loss of the cryptocurrency investments, the $10 million estate left by Alex is now worth less than half.

Not that Chelsea receives a single penny. Because JJ was the last to die, JJ's children inherit the entirety of the remaining estate. Chelsea no longer has access to any of the money that was being used to pay for her education, housing, books, personal items, or health insurance. Chelsea will have to figure out how to pay her tuition for next semester, not to mention the cost of attending graduate school.

Chelsea will have to rely on the generosity of her step-siblings, who, though they love Chelsea, are not too keen on sharing their inheritance.

> *Your choices created a situation in which your daughter receives no inheritance. Instead, everything you worked so hard for before your death is distributed to people you did not even know, lost, or paid to the government. Your daughter's future is left uncertain—but with different planning, this financial insecurity could have been avoided.*
>
> *To choose a different legacy, go back to the beginning of Story Two on page 70 and make different choices.*

ALEX DOES NOT REMARRY WITH THE WILLS PROVIDED BY MR. THOMAS

Heartbroken, Alex spends years trying to move forward and finds comfort only in work and your daughter, Chelsea. Alex, who works day and night and begins investing in cryptocurrency, turns the $3 million estate you built together into $10 million. Doctors say Alex should slow down, but work helps ease the pain of your death.

Alex never considers updating the will you executed together. After all, it clearly specifies your assets will be transferred to Chelsea upon both of her parents' deaths. This is exactly what Alex wants, so there seems to be no need to revisit Mr. Thomas. After your death, Mr. Thomas never said anything different.

Despite the tragedy of your death, Chelsea is a happy child, and she grows into a happy teenager. She does wish that Alex would spend less time at work and more time with her, but rather than complain, she copes by emulating Alex's workaholic mentality and earns high grades at school.

And then, sixteen years after your death, Alex dies. For those who knew Alex, this was not a big surprise. Alex was bound to have a heart attack, given the stress and fatigue associated with consistently working sixteen-hour days. In fact, since your death, Alex had not taken more than a few days of vacation.

Chelsea immediately shuts down upon Alex's death. Your sister-in-law Kaari, whom you and Alex named as guardian in your will, assumes custody of Chelsea. Kaari is a nurse who works evenings, which means Chelsea is often alone at night, and she feels lonely, devastated, and abandoned. Though your sister-in-law is committed to your daughter's happiness, she simply is not home enough to comfort Chelsea.

Kaari considers finding a different job, but the economy is unkind, and though she submits hundreds of résumés, her search is unsuccessful.

The only other option she can imagine is quitting her job to become a full-time parent, but she is disheartened to hear that your assets are going through the long and arduous probate court process.

Mr. Thomas' son, Kent Thomas Jr., has taken over the wills Mr. Thomas prepared for you. He explains to Kaari that Alex's assets will be tied up in court for at least a year and possibly as long as eighteen months. He explains probate is basically a lawsuit filed against Alex's estate for the benefit of Alex's creditors. It is a system the courts use to protect potential creditors of your estate and order the distribution of your assets.

Additionally, and what Kent Thomas Jr. couldn't know, half of Alex's estate was held in cryptocurrency accounts that were lost when Alex died because he didn't leave clear instructions about where they were or how to access them.

> When you buy cryptocurrency, your account or wallet can only be accessed by private keys. If those private keys are lost, your account is essentially gone. Nobody has access to it.
>
> With some crypto exchanges, such as Coinbase, the person named or appointed as the executor of your estate can show that paperwork to Coinbase and get access to the account, but only after going through the court process called "probate," which can take several months, or even years, and be quite expensive.
>
> To ensure your cryptocurrency assets are not lost, discuss your holdings with your Personal Family Lawyer and confirm your lawyer has included planning for the immediate transfer of and access to these assets upon your incapacity or death without court intervention.

Normally, Alex's life insurance would have paid out right away, but because Chelsea is not yet an adult and the life insurance was designated to her as the beneficiary, the court will have to designate a financial guardian for Chelsea before the life insurance can be distributed. Kent Thomas Jr. explains that the probate process could cost approximately 5 percent of the $5 million estate (or $250,000). Worst of all, because of Kaari's poor credit, she cannot get bonded (a bond is basically an insurance policy paid for by your estate in case the executor negligently squanders the estate) and will not be able to serve as the financial guardian. You and Alex named your parents as the financial guardians when you first created your wills so many years before, but your parents died five years earlier. The court will have to appoint an expensive professional guardian at $225 an hour.

Kaari struggles through the next year. She discovers Chelsea has not been coming home at night. Furthermore, Kaari suspects Chelsea has started drinking. Chelsea is no longer an honor student. She is obviously having problems.

Chelsea is three months away from turning eighteen.

During these three months, Chelsea and Kaari fight nonstop. Kaari wants Chelsea to stay living with her and continue therapy, but Chelsea refuses. She will soon be a millionaire, and she wants to live alone.

When she turns eighteen, Chelsea moves into an apartment of her own. Angry with Kaari, Chelsea cuts off all contact. Kaari has spent the last twenty-two months taking an emotional and financial beating while trying to care for Chelsea. Now, Kaari feels broken. She has no energy left to fight with, reason with, or save Chelsea from the destructive will of an eighteen-year-old with a seemingly endless stream of money. Kaari gives up and tries to put some semblance of a life back together for herself.

Left to her own devices and with what an eighteen-year-old would consider a large fortune, Chelsea rents a nice apartment and does not bother applying to any universities.

Instead, with high school finished and no reason to get a job, she spends more and more time with her friends. Perhaps unsurprisingly, with too much time on her hands, not enough structure in her life, and having lost both of her parents young, Chelsea soon marries a man about a decade older than her.

In a way, her husband is good for her. He is a little showy, drives expensive cars, buys fancy suits, and flashes money to impress people, but Nick is not a bad man. Nick is a clinical researcher in the biotech industry, which had always interested Chelsea. He provides some structure and maturity in her life, and Chelsea shifts her focus from partying to helping Nick in his business endeavors. She stops staying out late and begins to concentrate her energy on her home life and helping her husband.

Chelsea is not particularly educated or mature when it comes to finances, and she and Nick simply combine all their assets, as most couples do. Chelsea assumes from Nick's behavior that he has ample assets, and she leaves the family bookkeeping to him.

Like many marriages, Chelsea and Nick's relationship has its ups and downs. Within a few years of marrying, Chelsea starts questioning her relationship with Nick.

Does she seek a divorce? If so, turn to the section titled "Chelsea and Nick Divorce" on page 103. If not, turn to the section titled "Chelsea and Nick Remain Married" on page 105.

CHELSEA AND
NICK DIVORCE

As Chelsea ages, she also matures. Though she loves Nick, she wonders if she was too young to get married. She wants to attend college and pursue a career of her own. Nick, on the other hand, is not interested in having anything other than a stand-by-her-man wife. He wants to be with someone who will raise his children and support his career. Though Chelsea wants to do both of those things, she also wants to pursue her own independence.

After what seems like an endless stream of fights, Chelsea and Nick decide to divorce amicably. But the situation quickly turns ugly when Chelsea realizes Nick had few assets when he and Chelsea married. Instead, Nick spent a sizable chunk of Chelsea's inheritance. Because the couple combined their assets when they married, he also now gets half the inheritance you and Alex worked so hard to leave for Chelsea.

> Your daughter is left without both parents—and as a direct result of insufficient planning due to your naive faith in an attorney with out-of-date practices, she now faces an uncertain financial future. Everything you and your spouse wanted for your daughter is in jeopardy, with your legacy now left in the hands of a man who was not right for her. While you only wished the best for her, she is now alone in the world and financially worse off.
>
> But, of course, it didn't have to be this way. If this is not the life you want for Chelsea, return to the beginning of Story Two on page 70 and choose a different legacy.

CHELSEA AND NICK REMAIN MARRIED

As Chelsea ages, she also matures. Though she loves Nick, she wonders if she was too young to get married. She wants to attend college and pursue a career of her own. Nick, on the other hand, is not interested in having anything other than a stand-by-her-man wife. He wants to be with someone who will raise his children and support his career. Though Chelsea wants to do both of those things, she also wants to pursue her own independence.

After what seems like an endless stream of fights, Chelsea and Nick decide to seek counseling. Both are committed to making the marriage work, and as they progress and grow, they evolve into more mature, responsible adults who respect each other, growing a stronger relationship along the way.

Unfortunately, within several years of their marriage, Chelsea's husband is sued. Unbeknownst to him, one of Nick's biotech businesses had not obtained proper consent before harvesting tissue from donors. Because they have combined all their assets, most of Chelsea's inheritance is lost, satisfying several judgments against her husband.

Chelsea does her best to remain supportive throughout her husband's legal troubles. But the lawsuits have nearly driven the couple into bankruptcy, and Chelsea is forced to take a job rather than attend college. She is angry and bitter, and her and Nick's marriage begins to deteriorate.

Your daughter is left without both parents—and as a direct result of insufficient planning due to your naive faith in an attorney with out-of-date practices, she now faces an uncertain financial future. Everything you and your spouse wanted for your daughter is in jeopardy, with your legacy now left in the hands of a man who has made irresponsible decisions. While you only wished the best for her, her life is significantly worse than you—and she—envisioned.

Is this the life you want for your daughter? If not, go back to the beginning of Story Two on page 70 and choose a different legacy.

ALEX REMARRIES WITH A TRUST

Heartbroken, Alex spends several years trying to move forward and finds comfort only in work and your daughter, Chelsea. Alex works day and night, turning the $3 million you and Alex owned at the time of your death into $10 million by making some smart cryptocurrency investments alongside his earnings from work. Doctors say Alex should slow down, but work helps ease the pain of your death.

Luckily, Alex meets JJ, a co-worker and fellow work-first go-getter. JJ has sole custody of two children from a previous marriage. Eventually, JJ and Alex marry. Because they work so hard, they do not make time to think about planning, as most people do not. But the trust you and Alex established together requires Alex to have a prenuptial agreement with any new spouse or be cut off from access to the special protected trust created after your death.

Before marrying JJ, Alex calls Nat, your Personal Family Lawyer, who prepares a prenuptial agreement for Alex and JJ to sign.[7] JJ

---

7   JJ must have separate counsel to sign off on the prenuptial agreement. In California, as in many other states, a prenuptial agreement is only valid if each of the parties is represented by independent counsel. Contact a Personal Family Lawyer in your state for more guidance.

is more than happy to do so because it is required by your Life and Legacy Plan—not because Alex doesn't trust her.

While JJ and Alex are preparing for marriage and signing their prenuptial agreement, Nat prepares a trust for JJ and Alex's joint assets and a separate trust for the assets JJ brings into their marriage. Nat reminds Alex how to maintain the separate assets acquired during your marriage. Nat assures Alex that if anything happens to Alex, your assets will go to Chelsea, not JJ or JJ's children.

Although both JJ and Alex work too much, Chelsea and her two step-siblings are relatively happy and well-adjusted children. Alex and JJ are both good providers who want the best for all three children.

Alex and JJ are so focused on their careers, though, that they are somewhat neglectful and indifferent when it comes to providing emotional support and involvement, but the three step-siblings are close. And because Alex and JJ are so well off, the children are able to participate in many school activities and find support in extended networks of school friends, parents, coaches, teachers, and the like.

Then, sixteen years after your death, Alex dies. For those who knew Alex, this was not a big surprise. Alex was bound to have a heart attack, given the stress and fatigue associated with consistently working sixteen-hour days. In fact, since your death, Alex had not taken more than a few days of vacation.

Chelsea suffers tremendously over the loss of Alex. Luckily, she has loving step-siblings and a staunch support network through school and all of her extracurricular activities. She is also lucky to have JJ, who is committed, though benignly neglectful. Nevertheless, Chelsea cannot help but suffer from having lost both parents to untimely deaths. Moreover, despite all of their love and commitment, Chelsea cannot help but feel just a tiny bit like an outsider in her family now that both her biological parents are gone. She longs for people whose faces look like her own and who remember the inside jokes and little songs of her childhood.

Fortunately, there will be plenty of resources to provide Chelsea with therapeutic and other necessary support to move through her grief and emotional challenges. Ample money has been set aside in a trust specifically designated for Chelsea, and Nat is providing the trustee, your sister-in-law Kaari, with guidance on how to use the money for Chelsea's benefit. Chelsea is able to receive grief counseling, paid for by the trust, and JJ is able to receive payments for the care of Chelsea.

There is no need for the court process called "probate," and no estate taxes need be paid. Everything is handled in the privacy of Nat's office, and the trust funds are used for Chelsea as per the guidelines you and Alex thought out many years earlier.

Fortunately, Alex also worked with Nat to inventory and keep track of all of his assets, including the cryptocurrency accounts. Additionally, Alex left explicit instructions in his updated Life and Legacy Plan about how and where to access the "private keys" to the cryptocurrency accounts, so Nat is able to ensure those funds are not lost. Together, Alex and Nat made sure the trustee of the trust would get immediate access to those accounts in the event of Alex's incapacity or death.

When you buy cryptocurrency, your account or wallet can only be accessed by private keys. If those private keys are lost, your account is essentially gone. Nobody has access to it.

With some crypto exchanges, such as Coinbase, the person named or appointed as the executor of your estate can show that paperwork to Coinbase and get access to the account, but only after going through the court process called "probate," which can take several months, or even years, and be quite expensive.

To ensure your cryptocurrency assets are not lost, discuss your holdings with your Personal Family Lawyer and confirm your lawyer has included planning for the immediate transfer of and access to these assets upon your incapacity or death without court intervention.

The money in the trust is administered and supervised by Kaari, who was designated by you and Alex to act as trustee so long as she was not Chelsea's guardian.

Whenever possible, it is a good idea to name two separate people as guardian (responsible for your children's physical, emotional, and spiritual wellbeing) and trustee (responsible for your estate's financial wellbeing). This keeps checks and balances in place where the trustee and guardian watch over each other to ensure they are both acting in the best interests of your children.

Kaari, Alex's sister, simply ensures the money is used for its intended purpose: to care for Chelsea. JJ does not need to petition the court for access to the money. Instead, JJ and Kaari work out a regular schedule of trust distributions. JJ, as Chelsea's care guardian, makes requests to Kaari for extraordinary expenses, and Kaari promptly provides JJ with funds.

When Chelsea turns eighteen, she will be able to obtain funds directly from the trust with Kaari's approval. When she turns thirty, the trust that you and Alex created dictates Chelsea will be old enough to control trust monies on her own.

The more guidance you can provide your chosen trustee ("financial parent") about how you want trust assets distributed to your child and/ or their guardian, the better.

For most parents, this is hard to do. How do you even know where to start?

Let us make it easy for you.

Visit PersonalFamilyLawyer.com and download the free Trustee Distribution Guidelines worksheet. In this worksheet, you will walk through ten different types of life events you may want to consider supporting for your child, such as travel, career choices, weddings, businesses, and transportation. Plus, you will see three possible guidelines you can give a trustee; select one of the examples provided or use them to spark ideas to create your own.

Or better yet, work with a Personal Family Lawyer for guidance and support on how to establish your trust and provide guidelines to your trustee so you (and they) don't have to go it alone.

Because you structured the trust this way, Kaari is able to act as Chelsea's "financial parent" until Chelsea is mature enough to make her own financial decisions.

When Chelsea graduates from high school, she is able to attend the university of her choice. She maintained high grades in high school and had numerous sporting and other extracurricular activities on her résumé. Between the grants and scholarships she receives and the trust you and Alex set up for her, there are no limits on the amount Chelsea can spend pursuing higher education. She excels in the sciences, intends to attend graduate school, and ultimately wants a job in the field of biotechnology. Through the hard work of you and Alex, Chelsea has everything going for her.

Nevertheless, perhaps because she lost both parents so young, Chelsea ends up marrying young and to an older man, a clinical researcher she meets in one of the university's labs. Nick is a little showy, drives expensive cars, buys fancy suits, and flashes money to impress people. But he and Chelsea have similar interests, and Nick is a caring husband. He provides some structure and maturity in her life. Chelsea helps Nick in his business endeavors, and Nick helps Chelsea in her studies.

Because money is not an issue for Chelsea, she fails to discuss finances with Nick. But after graduating from college, Chelsea realizes several things about Nick. First, he has a mountain of debt and is up to his neck in credit card bills. He also lacks integrity in his business dealings. Unfortunately, within a few months of their marrying, Nick is sued because one of his biotech businesses was harvesting tissue without proper donor-consent forms. Nick's own assets are obliterated by the judgment, but because Chelsea's assets belong to the trust you set up for her, they are untouchable.

This experience, coupled with the wisdom that comes with age, causes Chelsea to begin questioning her marriage to Nick. Chelsea wants to pursue a career of her own, but Nick is not interested in having anything other than a stand-by-her-man wife. He wants to be with someone who will raise his children and support his career. Though Chelsea wants to do both of those things, she also wants to pursue her own independence.

Though she loves Nick, Chelsea wonders if she was rash in marrying him so young. After what seems like an endless stream of fights, Chelsea and Nick decide to divorce amicably. But the situation takes a twist when Nick tries to claim half of Chelsea's inheritance.

Chelsea's lawyer laughs when she hears the news. "Not a chance," Nat tells Nick. Nick's lawyer informs his client of the same. The money is protected by the trust you set up for Chelsea when she was just a little baby. Nick cannot touch it. Because her assets are held in trust, they cannot be reached by the divorce proceedings, and none of the money will be distributed to Chelsea's ex-husband as part of any dissolution settlement.

Chelsea is relieved when she hears the news. Ready for a fresh start, Chelsea can use the money in the trust to start a business or attend graduate school, whatever she chooses. While her marriage was definitely a setback in her life, Chelsea has the resources, education, and support network to move on and pursue her own dreams.

Continue to the section titled "Chelsea Goes to Graduate School" on page 121.

ALEX DOES NOT REMARRY
WITH A TRUST

Heartbroken, Alex spends years trying to move forward and finds comfort only in work and your daughter, Chelsea. Alex, who works day and night and begins investing in cryptocurrency, quickly turns the $3 million estate you built together into $10 million. Doctors say Alex should slow down, but work helps ease the pain of your death.

Despite the tragedy of your death, Chelsea is a relatively happy and well-adjusted child. She wishes Alex would spend more time at home with her, but rather than let it get her down, she decides to emulate Alex's workaholic ways, and she throws herself into schoolwork, sports, and other extracurricular activities. She excels in the sciences and someday wants to work in the biotech field.

But Chelsea's stability is shattered when Alex dies. For those who knew Alex, it was not a big surprise. Alex was bound to have a heart attack, given the stress and fatigue associated with consistently working sixteen-hour days. In fact, since your death sixteen years prior, Alex had not taken more than a few days of vacation.

Chelsea immediately shuts down upon Alex's death. Your sister-in-law Kaari, whom you and Alex named as guardian in your will, assumes custody of Chelsea. Kaari is a nurse who works evenings; however, it takes no time at all for her to realize that Chelsea cannot be left home alone at night. At first, it does not seem feasible for Kaari to quit working in order to become a full-time parent—though that may be what Chelsea needs right now—and she worries about finding a daytime job in the slow economy.

Thank goodness you and Alex learned about trusts from Nat, your Personal Family Lawyer. Almost immediately after Alex's death, Kaari calls Nat and learns she can get nearly instant access to all of the money in the trust to meet any of Chelsea's needs, including grief counseling, through the trustee you and Alex appointed to act as Chelsea's "financial parent."

Think of the trustee as your child's "financial parent" because this person will control distribution from the trust until your child is mature enough to make these decisions on their own. When possible, the trustee should be someone other than the guardian (who is responsible for taking care of your child's physical, emotional, and spiritual needs) to enrich the system with checks and balances. The trustee watches the guardian, who in turn watches the trustee. The trustee choice is critical in a successful distribution of trust funds. To download a free article on how to choose the right trustee, visit PersonalFamilyLawyer.com.

You and Alex named your best friend and Chelsea's godfather, Peter, to serve as trustee if Kaari was serving as Chelsea's guardian.

You initially figured you would name Kaari to be both the trustee and Chelsea's guardian, but Nat recommended you name two different people to act as guardian and trustee, if possible.

The great news is Kaari and Peter do not have to go through the court system to access your assets for Chelsea's benefit. Because of your smart planning, there is no need for the court process called "probate," and no estate taxes are due.

Fortunately, Alex also worked with Nat to inventory and keep track of all his assets, including the cryptocurrency accounts. Additionally, Alex left explicit instructions in his updated Life and Legacy Plan about how and where to access the "private keys" to the cryptocurrency accounts, so Nat is able to ensure those funds are not lost. Together, Alex and Nat made sure the trustee of the trust would get immediate access to those accounts in the event of Alex's incapacity or death.

> When you buy cryptocurrency, your account or wallet can only be accessed by private keys. If those private keys are lost, your account is essentially gone. Nobody has access to it.
>
> With some crypto exchanges, such as Coinbase, the person named or appointed as the executor of your estate can show that paperwork to Coinbase and get access to the account, but only after going through the court process called "probate," which can take several months, or even years, and be quite expensive.
>
> To ensure your cryptocurrency assets are not lost, discuss your holdings with your Personal Family Lawyer and confirm your lawyer has included planning for the immediate transfer of and access to these assets upon your incapacity or death without court intervention.

Everything is handled in the privacy of Nat's office, and the trust funds are used for Chelsea as per the guidelines you and Alex thought out many years earlier. As trustee, Peter is guided by Nat to work with Kaari as guardian and determine Chelsea's financial needs so the money in the trust is used for its intended purpose: to care for Chelsea.

Because you and Alex established the trust with clear directions that dictate its use, Kaari does not need to petition the court for access to the money. With the help of Nat, Kaari and Peter determine Chelsea needs a full-time parent. Until Chelsea turns eighteen, Peter distributes money from the trusts to cover Kaari and Chelsea's living expenses, allowing Kaari to work part time and be available for Chelsea during this emotional period in her life.

Later, after Chelsea turns eighteen, Peter will distribute money to Chelsea for college, transportation, a wedding, and other needs she may have until she is mature enough to make her own financial decisions. Peter is guided by the clear guidelines you documented with Nat's support years earlier.

With financial worries off of her back, Kaari is able to take the time to find a part-time day job in nursing. While Chelsea is at school, Kaari works, continuing to move her career forward while still spending evenings with Chelsea, who, with the help of a grief counselor, is slowly but steadily regaining her stability.

Although it is not easy, when Chelsea graduates from high school, she feels strong enough to attend a university. Despite the rough patch following Alex's death, she maintained high grades in high school. Between the grants and scholarships she receives and the trust you and Alex set up for her, there are no limits on the amount she can spend pursuing higher education.

The more guidance you can provide your chosen trustee ("financial parent") about how you want trust assets distributed to your child and/or their guardian, the better.

For most parents, this is hard to do. How do you even know where to start?

Let us make it easy for you.

Visit PersonalFamilyLawyer.com and download the free Trustee Distribution Guidelines worksheet. In this worksheet, you will walk through ten different types of life events you may want to consider supporting for your child, such as travel, career choices, weddings, businesses, and transportation. Plus, you will see three possible guidelines you can give a trustee; select one of the examples provided or use them to spark ideas to create your own.

Or better yet, work with a Personal Family Lawyer for guidance and support on how to establish your trust and provide guidelines to your trustee so you (and they) don't have to go it alone.

Nevertheless, perhaps because she lost both parents so young, Chelsea ends up marrying young and to an older man, a clinical researcher she met in one of the university's labs. Nick is a little showy, drives expensive cars, buys fancy suits, and flashes money to impress people. But he and Chelsea have similar interests, and Nick is a caring husband. He provides some structure and maturity in her life. Chelsea helps Nick in his business endeavors, and Nick helps Chelsea in her studies.

Because money is not an issue for Chelsea, she fails to discuss finances with Nick. But after graduating from college, Chelsea realizes several things about Nick. First, he has a mountain of debt and is up to his neck in credit card bills. He also lacks integrity in his business dealings. Unfortunately, within a few months of their marrying, Nick is sued because one of his biotech businesses was harvesting tissue without proper donor-consent forms. Nick's own assets are reached by the judgment, but because Chelsea's assets belong to the trust you set up for her, they are untouchable.

This experience, coupled with the wisdom that comes with age, causes Chelsea to begin questioning her marriage to Nick. Chelsea wants to pursue a career of her own, but Nick is not interested in having anything other than a stand-by-her-man wife. He wants to be with someone who will raise his children and support his career. Though Chelsea wants to do both of those things, she also wants to pursue her own independence.

Though she loves Nick, Chelsea wonders if she was rash in marrying him so young. After what seems like an endless stream of fights, Chelsea and Nick decide to divorce amicably. But the situation takes a twist when Nick tries to claim half of Chelsea's inheritance.

Chelsea's lawyer laughs when she hears the news. "Not a chance," Nat tells Nick. Nick's lawyer informs his client of the same. The money is protected by a trust, and Nick cannot touch it. Because her assets are held in trust, they cannot be reached by the divorce proceedings, and none will be distributed to her ex-husband as part of any dissolution settlement.

Chelsea is relieved when she hears the news. Ready for a fresh start, Chelsea can use the money in the trust to start a business or attend graduate school, whatever she chooses. While her marriage was definitely a setback in her life, Chelsea has the resources, education, and support network to move on and pursue her own dreams.

Continue to the section titled "Chelsea Goes to Graduate School" on page 121.

CHELSEA GOES TO GRADUATE SCHOOL

Chelsea is an avid learner, and she pursues a PhD in biomedical research. She later obtains her medical degree with a specialty in cardiology, an interest that likely stemmed from Alex's heart attack. After years and years of school, Chelsea is thrilled to start her own practice alongside Dr. Corbin, with whom she completed her fellowship and developed a romantic relationship.

Chelsea has chosen a high-risk profession. Immediately after their marriage, she and Dr. Corbin sit down with an attorney to discuss the liability insurance they must carry, as well as the proper structure to protect their business and assets from risk. Chelsea's attorney is impressed with the nearly bulletproof trust you and Alex established for her. The attorney explains its benefits: if either Chelsea or Dr. Corbin is sued, a likely occurrence in the medical profession, the judgment cannot reach Chelsea's assets. This means the money will be available for Chelsea and your grandchildren, who come a few years after Chelsea and Dr. Corbin marry. The lawyer explains the assets are further protected from any future spouses (Chelsea already knows about this!) or stepchildren, keeping the money for its intended recipients: your children and grandchildren.

Fortunately, Chelsea and her husband have a healthy medical practice and are never sued. They also have a healthy marriage and three children. Because of your wise planning, your grandchildren, and even their children, benefit from the trust's assets, which are forever protected from creditors, predators, lawsuits, and future spouses.

Chelsea often gathers her children around to listen to the recording you created many years before, when you met with your Personal Family Lawyer to plan for your life and legacy, which Nat preserved digitally and stored in the cloud. Chelsea and your grandchildren hear you and Alex talk about the life lessons you hoped to pass on and the love you felt for Chelsea. Despite Chelsea's grief at losing you, she and her children feel infinite peace and know everything will work out as it is supposed to, and they feel the loving embrace of an energy greater than themselves.

Congratulations. You made the deliberate choice to plan for your life and legacy, which had the lasting impact of not only increasing your whole family wealth for generations to come but also protecting your loved ones and ensuring they feel your love even after you are gone. You have left the world a better place for the people you love, and in turn, they are working to improve the world for countless others.

The Additional Resources section at the end of the book contains more information about creating a legacy for your family.

From the prior two stories, you now know how to protect your children's physical and financial wellbeing, but what about their emotional wellbeing? Turn to Story Three on page 124, where you will learn how to make decisions that will protect your adult children from any unnecessary emotional burden.

story three

YOU AND AIKO

NOT A LOT OF ASSETS, BUT A WHOLE LOT OF LOVE

You and Aiko are not wealthy—at least not on paper. You both come from working-class families. You met at a state university, which you paid for by taking modest student loans and living frugally. While you were there, some of your college friends complained that you never joined them for ski trips and dinners out. But you never had to explain to Aiko, and Aiko was just as eager as you were to find free activities. Together, you attended outdoor concerts, hiked for miles, went to poetry readings at local coffee shops, and listened to visiting speakers who came to the university. You and Aiko never had to pretend to be anything you were not, and it did not take long before you both knew you would always be each other's safe harbors.

With each other for support, you both obtained your degrees, quickly learning that college degrees do not equate to wealth. You always wanted to be a teacher, and Aiko approved, never suggesting another profession might be more lucrative. In return, you gave Aiko your wholehearted support to become a scuba instructor instead of taking a soul-sucking job in the business sector, even though Aiko did earn an MBA. Aiko loves animals and the environment, and the scuba position allows Aiko to spend twenty hours a week volunteering at the local animal shelter and for the local chapter of the Sierra Club.

Twenty years later, you have three children. Your twins, Olivia and Colin, attend high school in your neighborhood. Your eighteen-year-old son, Jet, is in his freshman year of college at the same state university you and Aiko attended. You and Aiko were the first members of your respective families to attend college, and although your families were supportive, they would have been equally happy if you had made other, less costly choices. You and Aiko are determined to foster a new tradition: all of your children will attend college (even if they ultimately choose careers as scuba instructors), and cost will be no obstacle for them.

Although you and Aiko still rent (who can afford to buy in Southern California?), you have managed to save about $150,000. In addition, you require your children to maintain good grades and take advantage of every extracurricular opportunity available. In that way, despite your modest incomes, you and Aiko hope to ensure all three of your kids earn college degrees. Indeed, Jet is currently attending college on a full academic scholarship.

So while you might not be rich on paper, you and Aiko feel wealthier than you ever would have imagined as children. You thank the Powers That Be that you met Aiko. As the old saying goes, "Two times one is not two but two thousand." Alone, you were two kids from working-class families struggling to make it through college on shoestring budgets. Alone, you had only limited family support. Alone, you felt like outsiders when the other students left for their spring break vacations. Together, you have created a comfortable, cultured home; raised three happy kids who will all attend college; and managed to save $150,000 while doing work you loved. When you think about the potential for your children's futures and for *their* children's futures, you smile deep inside.

For Christmas, you and Aiko decide to drive the family to Northern California to visit your parents, who are in an assisted living facility, and go skiing. You are lucky that Jet, despite being in his first year at the university, is still interested in spending time with the family. You want to take the opportunity for one last family vacation before Jet drifts away, as most young adults do before coming back as men. A ski vacation will be perfect: something your kids have rarely experienced and a welcome change from your family's usual activities.

Unfortunately, because you have lived in sunny Southern California all your lives, you and Aiko are unfamiliar with the weather in Northern California and have little understanding of how dangerous highway driving can be in the wintertime. You notice dark skies after you pass into Northern California. At first, your only concern is whether you will have nice weather on the slopes. Neither of you recognizes the threat posed by the clouds amassing over the snow-packed highway.

When the snowstorm hits, it destroys visibility, making it impossible to see even a few feet ahead of the car. The swirling snow blinds you to the road; in fact, you have no way of knowing whether you are still on the highway. You and Aiko want to pull over, but you are terrified of being hit by a similarly blinded driver behind you. Speaking in low murmurs, neither of you wants to let the kids realize how worried you are. Teeth clenched and hands white from gripping the steering wheel so hard, Aiko keeps driving, and together you press forward, trying to discern the road ahead. You are quickly exhausted, your backs ache, and your eyes start playing tricks on you from the strain. You want to cry, but pulling over seems as dangerous as continuing. You cannot remember the last time the kids said anything; despite your attempts to hide your worry, the kids are wide-eyed with concern.

And then, just like that, you drive out of the storm. The sky is still unremittingly gray, and the road is packed with snow, but at least you can see ahead. You breathe a collective sigh of relief and lean back in your seats. The kids start talking again. Aiko steps on the gas, and you do not object. The entire family is desperate to be done driving, out of the car, and checked into the lodge.

It happens without warning. As you cross an icy bridge, your Southern California tires simply lose their grip on the snow-packed highway below. Fishtailing uncontrollably, the car leaves the highway just at the end of the guard rail and takes a nose dive into the ditch ten feet below.

You are unconscious, and later, your children will learn that Aiko died instantly. Miraculously, none of the kids are seriously injured. Poor Jet is tested beyond his years, forced to leave you and the twins in the car while he searches for help or cell phone reception. Wearing his ski gear, he trudges the snowdrifts along-side the highway until he is able to flag down a truck driver.

You and Aiko are airlifted to a hospital while your kids are taken by ambulance to the same hospital. The authorities ask Jet about family members to call. He can't remember the name of your parents' assisted living facility, so he gives them your sister's name, and she is contacted and told to meet your children at the hospital. She replies that she will be there as soon as possible, but she has to fly in from New York where she was traveling on business, so she won't be there until the following day.

Until your sister arrives, Jet must deal with the authorities, the doctors, and the twins. The police take statements. The hospital asks about healthcare directives, medical records, and insurance. Jet is not sure what most of it means. He does not know what to do for his younger siblings, and he tries to maintain his composure until his aunt arrives or you awaken.

Your sister Teresa and her husband Mitch arrive the next afternoon. They too live in Southern California. When they arrive, the hospital informs them you still have not regained consciousness and your situation is critical. Mercifully, Teresa and Mitch relieve Jet's burden.

The hospital ombudsmen need to know about health insurance and health directives. The doctors need medical records in order to make competent decisions. The authorities need to know who will care for the twins, who are still minors. Your sister and her husband will do whatever is necessary to care for the children, but they feel too overwhelmed to make any immediate decisions. Everyone hopes you will regain consciousness and tell them what to do.

Finally, one of the ombudsmen prompts your sister gently, "Did they have wills? Or a trust? If so, a lot of the information we need might be found with those documents."

Do you and Aiko have wills? If so, turn to the section titled "You and Aiko Prepared Do-It-Yourself Wills" on page 131. Or do you and Aiko have a trust? If this is the case, turn to the section titled "You and Aiko Created a Trust" on page 171.

YOU AND AIKO PREPARED DO-IT-YOURSELF WILLS

"Yes." Your sister smiles wearily in relief. She finally knows the answer to a question. "They have wills."

When the kids were young, you and Aiko prepared do-it-yourself wills using a kit you found in a bookstore (this was before everything could be found for free on the internet). Your family always lived frugally, and you and Aiko did not believe you had the money to hire expensive lawyers. Besides, you were both intelligent, resourceful people and used to caring for yourselves. You read everything you could about estate planning, discussed the issues extensively, and meticulously filled in the forms in your kit.

You both agreed that if one of you died, your assets would be transferred to the other. When both of you died, your assets would be divided evenly among your three children. The kit had information about naming guardians for your children in your will, and you had both agreed on your sister Teresa.

After completing all the paperwork, you made copies of everything and gave them to Teresa and Mitch to be opened in an emergency.

"We have copies at home," Teresa tells the ombudsman. She tries to reach her neighbors so they can retrieve the documents and fax them to the hospital, but her neighbors are out of town for the holidays. The next day, she locates a friend who is able to drive to her house, locate the documents, and fax them to the hospital. At this point, you have been in the hospital for over forty-eight hours.

As soon as the documents arrive, Jet, Teresa, Mitch, and the hospital ombudsman sit down to review them. Included are copies of both your wills and your health insurance information.

Thankfully, your documents clearly provide a short-term guardian assignment stating your sister has the authority to care for your minor children. Teresa and Mitch will face no problems assuming guardianship of Olivia and Colin while you are incapacitated.[8]

But the more immediate question is how long that will be. How long will you remain unconscious at the hospital in Northern California, so far from home? You have plenty of health insurance, and you included all this information in the packet you gave Teresa and Mitch. But to make important decisions about your care, the hospital needs copies of your medical records and any healthcare directives you have created. Without such information, the hospital does not know about any medical conditions or drug allergies you may have, any medications you are already on that might interact adversely with proposed

---

8   Note that in most cases, a do-it-yourself kit or online estate plan will not include the full guardian nomination documents necessary to provide legal authority to care for minors, which we addressed thoroughly in Story One. In this story, we removed the issue by assuming the plan did include short-term guardian nominations, as would be included with a full Kids Protection Plan, so we can focus on other issues related to the failures of do-it-yourself planning solutions.

treatments, or any limitations on lifesaving measures you may have specified.

> Do your documents contain healthcare directives? If not, turn to the section titled "Your Documents Do Not Include Healthcare Directives" on page 135. If so, turn to the section titled "Your Documents Contain Healthcare Directives" on page 149.

YOUR DOCUMENTS
DO NOT INCLUDE
HEALTHCARE DIRECTIVES

You and Aiko drafted your wills with no expert assistance using a do-it-yourself kit. You followed all the directions and carefully discussed the issues you were directed to consider before meticulously completing the necessary paperwork. But you did not include healthcare directives, and even if you had, the directives may not have had the critical language needed to comply with Health Insurance Portability and Accountability Act (HIPAA) regulations.

> Among other things, HIPAA regulates the use and disclosure of health information. Intended to protect a person's privacy and keep medical information confidential, the federal law also hinders the transfer of critical information during emergencies. Due to stiff penalties for violations, medical professionals all but lock your medical records in an impenetrable vault.

Partly, the oversight was due to black-and-white thinking on your part; you assumed either you would be dead or you would be functioning well enough to make your own decisions. An in-between scenario never occurred to you, perhaps because you and Aiko figured one of you would always be around to make decisions for the other. But the omission was largely because the do-it-yourself kit you bought did not include healthcare-directive instructions.

After realizing you left no such directions, the hospital gently breaks the news to your family. Absent such directives, all decisions concerning your healthcare will fall on the shoulders of your eighteen-year-old son. It does not matter that your sister is better positioned to make such decisions; legally, the hospital must receive its instructions from Jet.

The lack of directives poses another problem. No one has any authorization to obtain your medical records, which are crucial to the hospital's ability to provide you appropriate care. To get them, the hospital must obtain authorization from Jet and complete arduous paperwork to comply with HIPAA, a well-intentioned but often cumbersome Congressional act meant, in part, to protect your privacy. Without HIPAA approval, the doctors must make their best guesses about your conditions and abstain from acting where the lack of knowledge could be dangerous.

Jet has only vague knowledge of your medical information. He tells the hospital administrative staff the name of your doctor, who is also Jet's doctor. Fortunately, Dr. Bowle treated you for all general health needs and is able to identify many of the specialists you saw. But although Jet, Teresa, the hospital, and Dr. Bowle all want the records transferred overnight, HIPAA interferes, and accessing the records takes time and red tape.

Despite the snail's pace, you still have not regained consciousness when the hospital finally gets Dr. Bowle's and your other providers' records. Maybe faster access to the records would have allowed more aggressive treatment early on and improved your chances. Maybe not.

No one will ever know.

Either way, the doctors are unable to stem the bleeding in your brain. You suffer irreversible brain damage. They do not believe you will ever regain consciousness. And even if you do, you will never have any meaningful cognitive function. You are being kept alive by machines, and the doctors believe you should be taken off life support. Ultimately, though, the choice will be left to your eighteen-year-old son.

Your family is devastated. Despite the doctors' warnings, they believed you would make a full recovery. Jet is being asked to make a decision no one, especially not an eighteen-year-old, is prepared to make. Your family asks for time to make a decision.

Teresa is your older sister by six years. She has known you your entire life. She knew you as a toddler, as a teenager, as a young adult, as an adult, and as a parent and spouse. She knew you as a friend and a confidante. When you scraped your knees, got yelled at by your father, and had a fist fight with your best friend, she comforted you. She thinks she knows everything about you. In her heart, she knows you would not want to be kept on life support indefinitely. After much soul-searching, Teresa knows you would want your family to let you go.

Jet is eighteen. He has known you his entire life. Every value, principle, and moral he holds came from you and Aiko. He thinks he knows everything about you. In his heart, he knows you would not want your family to give up. After much soul-searching, he knows you would want more time to fight.

Does your sister or your eighteen-year-old son really know what you would want? You did not provide any specific directions. If you had, their disagreement never would have arisen because your wishes would be the only ones that mattered.

Instead, for the next six months, you remain on life support while the situation between your sister and son deteriorates. They both have the best intentions. Your sister's heart breaks every time she sees you hooked up to all those machines while the life slowly drains from your body even as your spirit is prevented from finding peace. She knows it is irrational and unfair, but part of her begins to hate Jet for what he is doing to you.

Jet feels angry, hurt, resentful, and guilty. He knows what Teresa thinks—and deep down, he wonders if she is right. At the same time, he could never, under any circumstances, be the one to make the decision to let you go. If you had planned ahead, he never would have been burdened with this responsibility. And even though he knows it is irrational and unfair, part of him begins to hate Teresa for the way her doubts make him feel. Because contact with her causes his own doubts to gnaw away at him, he avoids her.

You are never stable enough to be moved back to Southern California, so most of the time, you are alone. Teresa and Mitch take the twins home. They let your rental go, move the twins into their house, and put most of your belongings into storage for the time being. Jet returns to the university. They all try to come regularly to see you, but the trip is long and expensive, and everyone is struggling financially; taking time away from work and school is challenging, to say the least.

Teresa and Mitch are wonderful people; otherwise, you and Aiko would not have chosen them as your first-choice guardians. Yet they are not well off. Mitch drives a delivery truck for a local beverage company, and Teresa works for a florist. Their own children are grown, and they have settled into a smaller home. They have no money set aside for two extra mouths. They do everything in their power to raise the twins in accordance with your wishes, but taking on two teenagers is a colossal burden.

Olivia and Colin both are involved in numerous extracurricular activities, all of which cost money. They are going through growth spurts and more than double the household consumption of food, not to mention energy and water costs. Olivia wears glasses, and Colin needs braces.

Even more importantly, Olivia and Colin need more than just financial support. They have just lost Aiko. You are in a permanently sedated condition in another part of the state. They have been moved into a new home, a home that does not feel permanent because they still believe you are going to regain consciousness. Their older brother is becoming increasingly hostile and withdrawn under the pressure forced on him. Everything is strange, unfamiliar, and in limbo.

Teresa and Mitch would like to move into a bigger house so some of your belongings can be brought out of storage. At least then, Olivia and Colin could have some familiar surroundings. They would like the twins to have their own rooms and a used car. They would like to fund some family activities for the twins and Jet. They would like Teresa to give up her weekend shifts at the shop so she can spend more time with the twins.

But they do not have the money to make all these changes overnight. Instead of cutting back on their hours at work, they are forced to take on extra shifts until they can get their new budget ironed out.

They sure could use the $150,000 you and Aiko put away. But although you and Aiko named guardians for your children, you did not execute the necessary documents to establish a trust and transfer your accounts into that trust, which would have allowed your named trustee to immediately access your bank accounts in the event of your incapacity.

Instead, your family must petition the court for a conservator to be appointed before any of them can access your assets. Teresa and Jet are in the process of getting a court-appointed guardian to oversee financial matters during your incapacity. The process is long and expensive, and the court-appointed guardian will charge at least $225 an hour.

You would have preferred your sister Teresa, the children's guardian, also be the guardian of your estate. But Teresa's weak credit and lack of assets prevent her from obtaining a bond (a bond is basically an insurance policy paid for by your estate in case the executor negligently squanders the estate), a necessary step in becoming an estate guardian unless expressly waived in writing, which was not explained in your do-it-yourself documents.

Besides, Jet mistrusts her and worries any control she has over the estate might somehow be used to gain an upper hand in the battle over your continued treatment. Add this mistrust to the normal red tape, and every step in the process takes time and involves conflict. Until you have a guardian of your estate, no one in the family has any access to your and Aiko's assets. Though your insurance is covering your healthcare costs, neither your three children nor the guardian you chose to raise the twins can access a single penny of the money you and Aiko saved.

Continue to the section titled "Guardian of the Estate" on page 143.

GUARDIAN OF THE ESTATE

Before the court can appoint a guardian, you die, and all the time spent petitioning to have an estate guardian appointed has been wasted. Instead, your estate will go through probate. Your will provides that your assets go in equal shares to your three kids. But when assets are distributed via a will, the estate must go through probate before anyone can access or distribute the assets. Probate is basically a lawsuit filed against your assets for the benefit of your creditors.

Probate is a system the courts use to determine exactly how much of your assets should be divided among your creditors and how much should go to your family. The probate process takes anywhere from a few months to more than a year (and can be even longer)—during which time your beneficiaries will have no access to your assets. Aggravating matters, your estate has to pay for a lawyer, court costs, appraisers, and other expenses.

So, having already been deprived of your assets for six months—during which time your sister and her husband have taken on the burden of caring for your teenage twins—your family must now wait another twelve to eighteen months to access your assets, which will be diminished by probate fees. The irony is you and Aiko did not have any creditors—a fact the court has no way of knowing until probate is complete.

At the completion of the probate process, your $150,000 estate is $10,000 lighter. Jet receives one-third, close to $47,000, outright and without any protection or direction.

You and Aiko raised Jet to understand money does not bring happiness. But even if you had not, Jet would find no joy in his inheritance. Jet is in a dark place. Since your death, Teresa and Mitch have tried to reach out to him and encourage him to spend time with his younger siblings.

But Jet suffered all of the normal anguish of losing both parents at once, and he feels your death was his fault. Away at the university and isolated by his conflict with Teresa, he does not know where to turn for help.

Instead, he immerses himself in music and painting, going hours without talking to anyone. He eats little and avoids his former friends. His paintings and music grow increasingly full of despair and loneliness. When the inheritance check comes, he is physically repulsed. Without talking to anyone, he immediately writes two checks: one half of his inheritance to your favorite charity and the other half to the local humane society where Aiko volunteered. Teresa does not find out about this decision for some time.

Because the twins are minors, they cannot receive their inheritances until they turn eighteen. Instead, the court holds onto their money until they reach adulthood. Teresa and Mitch can access the funds through the court-appointed guardian assigned at the conclusion of the probate process, but the guardian does not agree to make distributions for luxuries like after-school activities or family vacations.

Teresa and Mitch do get reimbursed for some of the money they spend on clothing and food but not for any of their lost work time or the little things they bought in the hope of providing you comfort while in the hospital.

When the twins turn eighteen, they each receive about $45,000 outright.

They are both graduating from high school and in the process of making decisions about college. Although they have suffered a terrible loss, including estrangement from their older brother, they have always had each other. They were lucky enough to make friends at their new high school, who helped them through their ordeal. Their aunt and uncle made them feel like welcomed additions to their home, shielding them from much of the conflict surrounding your medical decisions. Since you and Aiko had health insurance, the twins were even able to receive some counseling.

In many ways, they are normal eighteen-year-olds.

And this is precisely the problem. Olivia and Colin are normal eighteen-year-olds who have just been handed $45,000 apiece. To them, this money seems like a million dollars. Even $5,000, the amount they decide to give Teresa and Mitch, seems like a world of money. The twins are vaguely aware of the financial burden they have imposed on your sister and her husband, but because Teresa and Mitch tried to keep the twins from feeling any guilt, Olivia and Colin know very little about the actual costs incurred by their aunt and uncle. They do not know how much rent and groceries and utilities and car insurance cost.

They cannot imagine how their money could ever run out. They take loan and scholarship applications a little less seriously. As soon as he is installed in the dorms and away from the watchful eye of Teresa, Colin starts spending, buying clothes, books, expensive electronics, fancy cameras and phones, movies, and nights out.

Olivia, on the other hand, is interested in banking, and she decides to look into investment opportunities. She feels fortunate to meet Brian, a college student who befriends her instantly. Brian introduces her to an investment opportunity that promises to double her money in just a few months. Though Colin is distrustful of Brian, neither twin has the maturity or experience to recognize this "investment" for what it is: a scam.

Unbeknownst to both Olivia and Colin, the process of probate is public, and Brian "befriended" Olivia because he searched court records and found a target who would buy into his "investment" opportunity.

> Want to read Jacqueline Lee Bouvier Kennedy Onassis's will? How about the last will and testament of Elvis Presley? Wills are public record, which means any unscrupulous person who wants to marry for money or prey on recent inheritors with investment schemes can easily determine who has inherited large chunks of money. (To download copies of these wills, visit PersonalFamilyLawyer.com.)

By the end of their freshman year of college, both Colin's and Olivia's inheritances are gone. Colin squandered the money away, while Olivia was the victim of a predator.

Luckily, with the family's scant assets, the twins easily qualify for federally guaranteed student loans. They will graduate from college, but with over $50,000 in student loans each.

And what about your and Aiko's personal property? What becomes of that?

If you designated beneficiaries for your personal property, turn to the section titled "Your Will Designates Beneficiaries of Your Personal Property" on page 157. If not, turn to the section titled "Your Documents Do Not Contain Healthcare Directives and You and Aiko Did Not Specify Who Is to Receive Your Personal Property" on page 165.

YOUR DOCUMENTS CONTAIN HEALTHCARE DIRECTIVES

Thankfully, despite having created them yourselves without any expert help, you and Aiko included legally binding healthcare directives with the wills you prepared. As part of that process, you also executed HIPAA authorizations to allow your family to access your medical records and information. Your directives identify all your providers, allergies, and major medical conditions. In addition to appointing Teresa as the guardian of your children, your directives grant Teresa medical power of attorney and authorize her to obtain your medical records and make decisions for your healthcare. Your directives also provide, with great specificity, what sort of lifesaving measures you want and under what circumstances you want to be taken off life support.

Among other things, HIPAA regulates the use and disclosure of health information. Intended to protect a person's privacy and keep medical information confidential, the federal law also hinders the transfer of critical information during emergencies. Due to stiff penalties for violations, medical professionals all but lock your medical records in an impenetrable vault.

Teresa and her husband take charge immediately. Teresa is able to have all your medical records faxed to the hospital within hours, and the hospital uses the information to make immediate and competent decisions about how to move forward with your treatment. Your children are never faced with the burden of making any medical decisions for you, not even Jet, who is your closest living adult relative.

For the first week, your family members stay at a nearby hotel. At the end of the week, the doctors sit Teresa and Mitch down. Unable to stem the bleeding in your brain, the doctors fear you have suffered irreversible brain damage. They do not believe you will ever regain consciousness. And even if you do, you will never have any meaningful cognitive function. Based on your directives, the doctors believe you should be taken off life support.

Teresa is devastated. Despite the doctors' warnings, she had hoped you would make a full recovery. She feels overwhelmed by the burdens that have been placed on her. Three children are relying on her to tell them what to do next. Now, the doctors are asking her to make a decision about your very life. She asks them to give her twenty-four hours to make a decision.

Teresa is your older sister by six years. She has known you your entire life. She knew you as a toddler, as a teenager, as a young adult, as an adult, and as a parent and spouse. She knew you as a friend and a confidante. When you scraped your knees, got yelled at by your father, and had a fist fight with your best friend, she comforted you. She thinks she knows everything about you. In her heart, she believes you would not want to be kept on life support indefinitely. After much soul-searching, she knows you would want your family to let you go. Everything in your directives confirms what she believes.

The next day, she tells the doctors her decision.

Of your children, only Jet has any understanding that their aunt is involved in making such a decision. The twins are completely shielded. Jet knows more, but because the doctors, Teresa, Mitch, and your directives are all in agreement, he does not question the decision.

Teresa and Mitch arrange to have your bodies transported home so the joint funeral can take place in your town. Teresa and Mitch take your kids home with them. After the funeral, they send Jet back to college. They let your rental go, move the twins into their house, and put most of your belongings into storage until everyone can go through them together.

Teresa and Mitch are wonderful people; otherwise, you and Aiko would not have chosen them as your first-choice guardians. Yet they are not well off. Mitch drives a delivery truck for a local beverage company, and Teresa works for a florist. Their own children are grown, and they have settled into a smaller home. They have no money set aside for two extra mouths. They do everything in their power to raise the twins in accordance with your wishes, but taking on two teenagers is a colossal burden.

Olivia and Colin both are involved in numerous extracurricular activities, all of which cost money. They are going through growth spurts and more than double the household consumption of food, not to mention energy and water costs. Olivia wears glasses, and Colin needs braces.

Even more importantly, Olivia and Colin need more than just financial support. They have just lost both their parents and been moved into a new home. Many of their belongings and familiar surroundings are temporarily in storage. They feel disconnected from and alien to everything around them.

Teresa and Mitch would like to move into a bigger house so some of your belongings can be brought out of storage. At least then, Olivia and Colin can have some familiar surroundings. They would like the twins to have their own rooms and a used car. They would like to fund some family activities for the twins and Jet. They would like Teresa to give up her weekend shifts at the shop so she can spend more time with the twins.

But they do not have the money to make all these changes overnight. Instead of cutting back on their hours at work, they both take on extra shifts until they can get their new budget ironed out. They do the best they can. They make sure to reach out to Jet, even though he is technically an adult, doing everything within their power to keep Jet and his younger siblings in close contact.

They sure could use the $150,000 you and Aiko put away.

Your will provides that your assets go in equal shares to your three kids. But when assets are distributed via a will, the estate must go through probate before anyone can access or distribute the assets. Probate is basically a lawsuit filed against your assets for the benefit of your creditors.

Probate is a system the courts use to determine exactly how much of your assets should be divided among your creditors and how much should go to your family. The probate process takes anywhere from a few months to more than a year (and can be even longer)—during which time your beneficiaries will have no access to your assets. Aggravating matters, your estate has to pay for a lawyer, court costs, appraisers, and other expenses.

So, having already been deprived of your assets for six months—during which time your sister and her husband have taken on the burden of caring for your youngest children—your family must now wait another twelve to eighteen months to access your assets, which will be diminished by probate fees. The irony is you and Aiko did not have any creditors—a fact the court has no way of knowing until probate is complete.

After eighteen months, your $150,000 has been reduced to about $140,000. Jet receives one-third, almost $47,000, outright. You and Aiko raised him to understand money does not bring happiness. But even if you had not, Jet would find no joy in his inheritance. He contacts Teresa and Mitch and asks them to take the money and use it to care for the twins. Teresa and Mitch thank him profusely but tell him they will open a savings account with the money, which Jet can access later. Jet assures them he will never want the money, but Teresa and Mitch suspect this might change, knowing he can use the money for a down payment on a house or an emergency of his own. Not knowing much about money, Teresa and Mitch put the money in a regular savings account, earning a measly 0.5 percent interest rate.

Because the twins are minors, they cannot receive their inheritance until they turn eighteen. Instead, the court holds onto their money until the twins reach adulthood. Teresa and Mitch finally can ask to access the funds through the court-appointed guardian assigned at the conclusion of the probate process, but the guardian does not agree to make distributions for luxuries like after-school activities or family vacations. Teresa and

Mitch do get reimbursed for some of the money they spend on clothing and food but not for any of their lost work time or ancillaries they bought in the hope of providing you comfort while you were hospitalized.

In your documents, you and Aiko named Teresa the executor of your wills. She would have been able to take care of everything without a court-appointed guardian and make decisions about how funds are spent for the benefit of the twins, but your wills did not waive the bond required for someone to become an executor.

That means Teresa has to qualify to be bonded (a bond is basically an insurance policy paid for by your estate in case the executor negligently squanders the estate), and because of her weak credit, she does not qualify.

This is not what you wanted, but your do-it-yourself kit did not mention anything about bond provisions or how to waive bond.

Teresa and her husband, who have so generously cared for your twins for the past two years, never get access to any of the money you and Aiko set aside. Desperate, and with his permission, they access some of the money they had intended to hold onto for Jet.

When the twins turn eighteen, they each receive about $45,000 outright.

Olivia and Colin are graduating from high school and in the process of making decisions about college. Although they have suffered a terrible loss, they have always had each other. They were lucky enough to make friends at their new high school, who helped them through their ordeal. Their aunt and uncle made them feel like welcomed additions to their home. Since you and Aiko had health insurance, the twins were even able to receive some counseling.

In many ways, they are normal eighteen-year-olds.

And this is precisely the problem. Olivia and Colin are normal eighteen-year-olds who have just been handed $45,000 apiece. To them, this money seems like a million dollars. Even $5,000, the amount they decide to give Teresa and Mitch, seems like a world of money. The twins are vaguely aware of the financial burden they have imposed on your sister and her husband, but because Teresa and Mitch tried to keep the twins from feeling any guilt, Olivia and Colin know very little about the actual costs incurred by their aunt and uncle. They do not know how much rent and groceries and utilities and car insurance cost.

They cannot imagine how their money could ever run out. They take loan and scholarship applications a little less seriously. As soon as he is installed in the dorms and away from the watchful eye of Teresa, Colin starts spending, buying clothes, books, expensive electronics, fancy cameras and phones, movies, and nights out.

Olivia, on the other hand, is interested in banking, and she decides to look into investment opportunities. She feels fortunate to meet Brian, a college student who befriends her instantly. Brian introduces her to an investment opportunity that promises to double her money in just a few months. Though Colin is distrustful of Brian, neither twin has the maturity or experience to recognize this "investment" for what it is: a scam.

Unbeknownst to both Olivia and Colin, the process of probate is public, and Brian "befriended" Olivia because he searched court records and found a target who would buy into his "investment" opportunity.

By the end of their freshman year of college, both Colin's and Olivia's inheritances are gone. Colin squandered the money away, while Olivia was the victim of a predator.

Luckily, with the family's scant assets, the twins easily qualify for federally guaranteed student loans. They will graduate from college, but with over $50,000 in student loans each.

The twins, who were cared for so generously by their aunt and uncle, squander most of their money. Jet, who placed very little burden on his aunt and uncle, gave them his share because he was reluctant to use it.

And what about your and Aiko's personal property? What becomes of that?

If you designated beneficiaries for your personal property, turn to the section titled "Your Will Designates Beneficiaries of Your Personal Property" on page 157. If not, turn to the section titled "Your Will Does Not Designate Beneficiaries of Your Personal Property" on page 161.

YOUR WILL DESIGNATES BENEFICIARIES OF YOUR PERSONAL PROPERTY

About six months after the accident, while Jet is on break, your family gets together to go through your personal belongings.

While your family is very close, each of your children is an individual with their own interests, quirks, and soft spots. Each inherited characteristics unique to you, and each inherited characteristics unique to Aiko. While you were alive, you loved seeing the melding that made you and Aiko such an unbreakable team.

Like Aiko, Jet loves animals. While the twins probably barely noticed them on the bookshelf, Jet loved the little menagerie of ceramic, glass, stone, wooden, and even plastic animals Aiko amassed. Other people might have eventually thrown away the silly wind-up plastic frog and duck, but Aiko never had been able to throw away an animal and added every silly one they found to the menagerie. The twins never commented on them, but Jet loved each of them since he was a baby, treasuring the additions as much as Aiko.

Olivia, on the other hand, loves books. She jealously guards every book she has ever been given. Even as a toddler, she pretended to read your old college textbooks. She always asks for books for gifts, and if other family members are not careful, she hoards their neglected books in her own room. If you ever thought about taking any of your old books to Goodwill, Olivia wanted them for herself. Her room is lined with bookshelves, and she swears she has read every one of them.

Colin loves photography. He uses his allowance to buy photography books, and he loves the framed photographs you and Aiko used to decorate your walls. None of the art is expensive, but Colin loves it all and wants to take pictures like that himself one day. He loves your Pentax LX, and when you were alive, he begged you to let him take pictures with it.

Because you thought about it ahead of time, you and Aiko specified, to the extent possible, who should receive all your personal belongings. Jet gets the first choice of anything animal related. Olivia gets first choice of any books, and Colin has dibs on photographic art and equipment. Your sister gets all your kitchenware. Mitch gets the tools and lawn equipment. You left stories about a few items that were particularly important to you or you received from your parents or grandparents. These special items are sure to become family heirlooms handed down with loving care and stories from generation to generation.

Although it is bittersweet, your family is able to bond a little over their experience at the storage facility. They open boxes together and then check your will to see who is supposed to receive each item. They are able to share memories about you and Aiko related to your belongings. They remark upon particularly fitting designations. Some items are from your childhood and came to you through your parents. Teresa is able to share stories about your childhood with the kids, many of which they have never heard, and they hear the love in her voice as she talks about you.

Several items are not designated for anyone, but because each person thoughtfully has been given what mattered most, they are generous and honest with each other regarding the undesignated items. In the end, they all agree on boxes to be delivered to neighbors, other relatives, and local charities. They all feel a sense of catharsis from the day and closer as a family.

> In the end, your family will be okay. But by not making all your own choices in life, you left your children's futures vulnerable to poor choices by themselves and others.
>
> Are you completely satisfied with this outcome? If not, go back to the beginning of Story Three on page 124 and make different choices.

YOUR WILL DOES NOT DESIGNATE BENEFICIARIES OF YOUR PERSONAL PROPERTY

About six months after the accident, while Jet is on break, your family gets together to go through your personal belongings.

While your family is very close, each of your children is an individual with their own interests, quirks, and soft spots. Each inherited characteristics unique to you, and each inherited characteristics unique to Aiko. While you were alive, you loved seeing the melding that made you and Aiko such an unbreakable team.

Like Aiko, Jet loves animals. While the twins probably barely noticed them on the bookshelf, Jet loved the little menagerie of ceramic, glass, stone, wooden, and even plastic animals Aiko amassed. Other people might have eventually thrown away the silly wind-up plastic frog and duck, but Aiko never had been able to throw away an animal and added every silly one they found to the menagerie. The twins never commented on them, but Jet loved each of them since he was a baby, treasuring the additions as much as Aiko.

Olivia, on the other hand, loves books. She jealously guards every book she has ever been given. Even as a toddler, she pretended to read your old college textbooks. She always asks for books for gifts, and if other family members are not careful, she hoards their neglected books in her own room. If you ever thought about taking any of your old books to Goodwill, Olivia wanted them for herself. Her room is lined with bookshelves, and she swears she has read every one of them.

Colin loves photography. He uses his allowance to buy photography books, and he loves the framed photographs you and Aiko used to decorate your walls. None of the art is expensive, but Colin loves it all and wants to take pictures like that himself one day. He loves your Pentax LX, and when you were alive, he begged you to let him take pictures with it.

Unfortunately, you and Aiko did not think to specify beneficiaries for your personal property. If you had, you could have made sure the important things went to the right people and that each child got those possessions that best reflect the qualities they inherited from you both.

As it is, all the kids are uncomfortable. They know the purpose of the day is to divide your belongings between them. They know you and Aiko rejected materialism and valued generosity. The concept of divvying up your possessions makes them feel guilty.

Teresa and Mitch sense the children's reticence but are unsure how to put the three kids at ease. They become unduly deferential themselves.

On the one hand, everyone wants to be polite and give everyone else a first choice. On the other hand, the children feel they are being insensitive if they do not want certain things. The children feel caught between showing too much interest in certain things and too little in others. Perversely, the more they want something, the more they feel they should let someone else have it. And the more they do not want something, the more they feel they are disrespecting your memories if they turn it down.

Teresa, for her part, has sentimental connections to some of the items from your childhood or that came to you from your parents. Teresa would like to claim some of those for herself, but she feels reluctant to speak up in front of your children, who are so clearly uneasy with this process. And Mitch recognizes the worth of some of the larger household goods. As the person most removed from the uncomfortable family dynamics around him, Mitch is the most able to make practical choices.

The first box contains books. Olivia has already co-opted so many of your books that she feels she should give others a chance. She takes a few for herself. Jet and Colin are not that interested in most of the books, but they feel they are supposed to take some anyway. Is it insensitive to turn down books that belonged to you and Aiko? Are they supposed to keep them for sentimental reasons? Unsure and completely unaware anyone else genuinely might want these books, Jet and Colin each claim a handful.

A little later, the box with Aiko's menagerie is opened. Jet immediately bursts into tears and retreats. He wants them, but more than that, he wants Aiko. He wants not to have kept driving on that snowy day. He can barely talk. The others, unsure how to respond, continue their stiff division of items, each taking a few pieces of the menagerie and setting a couple aside for Jet. It does not occur to him to protest.

When a box containing your photographic equipment is opened, Colin immediately offers it to everyone else. To him, it is the most valuable possession you owned, not for its dollar worth, but because he loved using it and cherishes his memories of the time you spent together trying to take star shots and pictures of raindrops bouncing off leaves. Because Colin attributes such value to the equipment, he feels particularly compelled to be generous with it to the others. Mitch recognizes the dollar worth of the equipment, and when no one else seems to express any interest, he takes it.

In the end, everyone walks away with some important and sentimental pieces. The remainders are packed for neighbors with young children, other relatives, and your and Aiko's favorite charities. But what could have been a cathartic, bittersweet day of shared memories instead was an experience your family wants to forget. Their enjoyment of these items always will be slightly marred by the distinctly unpleasant and uncomfortable experience of rationing them to each other.

In the end, your family will be okay. But by failing to make clear all of your own choices in life, you left your hopes and wishes for the future vulnerable to poor choices by others.

Are you completely satisfied with this outcome? If not, go back to the beginning of Story Three on page 124 and make different choices.

YOUR DOCUMENTS DO NOT CONTAIN HEALTHCARE DIRECTIVES AND YOU AND AIKO DID NOT SPECIFY WHO IS TO RECEIVE YOUR PERSONAL PROPERTY

About six months after the accident, while Jet is on break, your family gets together to go through your personal belongings.

While your family is very close, each of your children is an individual with their own interests, quirks, and soft spots. Each inherited characteristics unique to you, and each inherited characteristics unique to Aiko. While you were alive, you loved seeing the melding that made you and Aiko such an unbreakable team.

Like Aiko, Jet loves animals. While the twins probably barely noticed them on the bookshelf, Jet loved the little menagerie of ceramic, glass, stone, wooden, and even plastic animals Aiko amassed. Other people might have eventually thrown away the silly wind-up plastic frog and duck, but Aiko never had been able to throw away an animal and added every silly one they found to the menagerie. The twins never commented on them, but Jet loved each of them since he was a baby, treasuring the additions as much as Aiko.

Olivia, on the other hand, loves books. She jealously guards every book she has ever been given. Even as a toddler, she pretended to read your old college textbooks. She always asks for books for gifts, and if other family members are not careful, she hoards their neglected books in her own room. If you ever thought about taking any of your old books to Goodwill, Olivia wanted them for herself. Her room is lined with bookshelves, and she swears she has read every one of them.

Colin loves photography. He uses his allowance to buy photography books, and he loves the framed photographs you and Aiko used to decorate your walls. None of the art is expensive, but Colin loves it all and wants to take pictures like that himself one day. He loves your Pentax LX, and when you were alive, he begged you to let him take pictures with it.

Unfortunately, you and Aiko did not think to specify beneficiaries for your personal property. If you had, you could have made sure the important things went to the right people—that each child got those possessions that best reflect the qualities they inherited from you both.

As it is, all the kids are uncomfortable. The distance between Jet and Teresa has grown, and the twins and Jet have been distant as a result. They know the purpose of the day is to divide your belongings between them. They know you and Aiko rejected materialism and valued generosity. The concept of divvying up your possessions makes them feel guilty.

Teresa and Mitch sense the children's reticence but are unsure how to put the three kids at ease. And they too are uncomfortable because of their recent conflict with Jet. So they become unduly deferential themselves.

On the one hand, everyone wants to be polite and give everyone else a first choice. On the other hand, the children feel they are being insensitive if they do not want certain things. The children feel caught between showing too much interest in certain things and too little in others. Perversely, the more they want something, the more they feel they should let someone else have it. And the more they do not want something, the more they feel they are disrespecting your memories if they turn it down.

Teresa, for her part, has sentimental connections to some of the items from your childhood or that came to you from your parents. Teresa would like to claim some of those for herself, but she feels reluctant to speak up in front of your children, who are so clearly uneasy with this process. And Mitch recognizes the worth of some of the larger household goods. As the person most removed from the uncomfortable family dynamics around him, Mitch is the most able to make practical choices.

The first box contains books. Olivia has already co-opted so many of your books that she feels she should give others a chance. She takes a few for herself. Jet and Colin are not that interested in most of the books, but they feel they are supposed to take some anyway. Is it insensitive to turn down books that belonged to you and Aiko? Are they supposed to keep them for sentimental reasons? Unsure and completely unaware anyone else might genuinely want these books, Jet and Colin each claim a handful.

A little later, the box with Aiko's menagerie is opened. Jet immediately bursts into tears and retreats. He wants them, but more than that, he wants Aiko. He wants not to have kept driving on that snowy day. He wants not to have been the one to make medical decisions for you. He wants not to have isolated himself from the twins and fought with Teresa. He is so torn up he cannot talk. The others, unsure how to respond, continue their stiff division of items, each taking a few pieces of the menagerie and setting a couple aside for Jet.

Jet will never be the same.

When a box containing your photographic equipment is opened, Colin immediately offers it to everyone else. To him, it is the most valuable possession you owned, not for its dollar worth, but because he loved using it and cherishes his memories of the time you spent together trying to take star shots and pictures of raindrops bouncing off leaves. Because Colin attributes such value to the equipment, he feels particularly compelled to be generous with it to the others. Mitch recognizes the dollar worth of the equipment, and when no one else seems to express any interest, he takes it, not because he is greedy, but because he does not want such valuable equipment to be donated to a stranger. Jet, who is suspicious of anything Teresa and Mitch do, misreads Mitch's intent. *He's out to get his greedy little hands on everything valuable,* Jet thinks as Mitch innocently adds the camera equipment to his pile.

And then the unthinkable happens. As Teresa stands to stretch, she accidentally steps on one of Aiko's glass animals, breaking it into three pieces. Jet has hit a breaking point.

He explodes. Hateful, vindictive, and hurtful words come flooding out of his mouth. Jet yells at Teresa that he hates her. He accuses her of wanting you dead. Then he turns to Mitch and says, "Mom and Dad never liked you. They never thought you were good enough for Teresa. But they were wrong. The two of you greedy monsters are perfect for one another."

Of course, none of this is true, but in the depths of his grief and pain, it feels true. The twins, unsure what to believe, try to quell the storm. This only makes Jet angrier. All the pain Jet has felt turns to blind rage as he accuses Colin and Olivia of disrespecting your memory. Colin fights back tears, but Olivia, tired of her older brother's attitude, fights back.

"Don't blame us! You're the one who made the decisions! You're the reason the suffering lasted so long!" she screams.

Jet's face freezes. His baby sister just confirmed his deepest fears. With Olivia, Colin, Mitch, and Teresa staring at him, Jet feels more alone than ever. Slowly, he picks up his belongings, turns, and leaves. No one stops him.

Your family will never be the same.

In silence, your sister, brother-in-law, and twin children pack the remaining items into boxes for neighbors, other relatives, and your and Aiko's favorite charities. In the end, everyone walks away with some important and sentimental pieces. But what could have been a cathartic, bittersweet day of shared memories instead was an experience your family wants to forget. Their enjoyment of these items always will be marred by Jet's outburst and the distinctly unpleasant and uncomfortable experience of rationing them to each other.

Your family has been battered by the tragedy of your death. Jet, Colin, and Olivia will never be close again. By not making your own choices in life, you left your wishes and hopes for the future vulnerable to poor choices by others. Maybe your family will recover, but they will forever be marked not just by the loss of their loved ones but the loss of the comfort and security in their remaining family members.

If you would never want this outcome for your family, go back to the beginning of Story Three on page 124 and make different choices.

YOU AND AIKO
CREATED A TRUST

"Yes." Your sister smiles wearily. She is happy to finally know the answer to a question. "They have a trust."

When your children were young, you and Aiko created an estate plan. Your family always lived frugally, and you and Aiko did not have the money to hire expensive lawyers. You were both intelligent, resourceful people, and you were used to caring for yourselves, so you intended to create do-it-yourself wills using a kit from a bookstore. But in the end, you decided your children's futures were too important to handle informally, and you hired a lawyer with a flexible payment plan to ensure you got the guidance you wanted.

It was worth every penny. You and Aiko at first thought the process would be simple. "We want our assets divided between our three children equally."

"What if they are still minors?" Ricardo, your Personal Family Lawyer, asked. "Do you want your minor children to receive their inheritances outright, or would you rather they receive it at an age-appropriate time designated by you? Or even better, in a lifetime protected trust?"

"Isn't that for rich kids?" you and Aiko asked, laughing a little in embarrassment at the size of your puny estate. Ricardo reassured you that you were making an appropriate decision, explaining that trusts used to be reserved solely for people with large assets but were being used more and more commonly by people who simply want to avoid probate; ensure their families have easy, immediate, and private access to their assets; and protect their young children from unwise spending.

Ricardo continued, "A trust is just an agreement and set of instructions between the one who has the money to put into the trust—called the 'grantor,' 'trustor,' 'settlor,' or 'trust maker'—and the trustee. The agreement is that the trustee will hold the property and follow the customized guidelines or instructions set out by the grantor for the benefit of the beneficiary.

"During your life, the trust creator—that's you—is the grantor, the trustee, and the beneficiary and does not give up control of any assets by putting them into the trust. Before your death, you determine who will serve as a successor trustee after your death and who the beneficiaries will be."

Aiko asked why a will was not sufficient, and Ricardo explained that if assets are passed through a will, the estate has to go through a lengthy and costly court process that prevents your family from reaching your assets at the time it needs them most: right after your death. And worst of all, the process is totally public, meaning any predator can find the names of the heirs to your estate.

"Probate" is the name of that court process. At the end of it, your assets and money are legally transferred to your heirs, but not until the court determines whether creditors have any claims to the estate. In addition to costing the estate about 5 percent of its worth, probate takes a minimum of twelve to eighteen months in California, and in some cases, it can be even longer.

"On the other hand," Ricardo continued, "if your assets are held in trust, they are not in your name and thus would not have to go through probate. That way, after your death, your children, beneficiaries, trustee, and guardian would be able to access your assets immediately, without having to wait through and pay for the probate process. In addition, the trust assets and distributions would be totally private. No one but your children and their guardians would ever know how much your children inherited or when they would get it."

You and Aiko really loved knowing you could make everything as easy as possible for the people you loved. Making sure you were never a burden on anyone was one of your greatest values.

While Teresa and her husband, Mitch, were chosen as guardians of your minor children, in the event of your death, Aiko's cousin Janice was chosen as guardian of the estate. Janice was the person you trusted most with financial responsibilities. Janice had good common sense and organizational skills. Though Janice was not a financial advisor, nor did she have extraordinary investment skills, you knew Janice would hire a trusted advisor and seek guidance from your Personal Family Lawyer.

Wherever possible, it is a good idea to name two separate people as guardian (responsible for your children's physical, emotional, and spiritual wellbeing) and trustee (responsible for your estate's financial wellbeing). This keeps checks and balances in place where the trustee and guardian watch over each other to ensure they are both acting in the best interests of your children.

Ricardo talked to you about all kinds of issues you never would have thought of on your own. With your lawyer's guidance, you considered what would happen in the event of your death or incapacity while your children were still minors. Who would you want to make medical decisions for you if you were unable to make them for yourself? And what sort of guidelines would you want that person to follow? You compiled lists of your medical providers, conditions, and allergies and executed HIPAA authorizations so your family would be able to obtain your medical records, if needed.

When the hospital ombudsman asks if Teresa has access to your medical records, she knows exactly whom to call. Your Personal Family Lawyer faxes copies of your medical records and healthcare directive to the hospital immediately, and the hospital receives everything within minutes of Teresa's request. As soon as the documents arrive, Jet, your sister, her husband, and the hospital administration sit down to review them.

Thankfully, the documents clearly provide that your sister has legal authority to care for your minor children. Teresa and Mitch will have no problems assuming legal guardianship while you are incapacitated.

The more immediate question is how long you will be incapacitated. How long will you remain unconscious at the hospital, so far from home? You have plenty of health insurance, and you included all of that information in the packet you gave Teresa and Mitch.

In addition to appointing Teresa as the guardian of your children, your directives grant Teresa medical power of attorney and authorize her to obtain your medical records and make decisions for your healthcare. Your directives also provide, with great specificity, what sort of lifesaving measures you want and under what circumstances you want to be taken off life support.

Teresa and her husband take charge immediately, and the hospital is able to use your medical records to make immediate and competent decisions about how to move forward with your treatment. Your children are never faced with the burden of making any medical decisions for you, not even Jet, who is your closest living adult relative.

For the first week, your family members stay at a nearby hotel. At the end of the week, the doctors sit Teresa and Mitch down. Unable to stem the bleeding in your brain, the doctors fear you have suffered irreversible brain damage. They do not believe you will ever regain consciousness. And even if you do, you will never have any meaningful cognitive function. Based on your directives, the doctors believe you should be taken off life support.

Teresa is devastated. Despite the doctors' warnings, she had hoped you would make a full recovery. She feels overwhelmed by the burdens that have been placed on her. Three children are relying on her to tell them what to do next. Now the doctors are asking her to make a decision about your very life. She asks them to give her twenty-four hours to make a decision.

Teresa is your older sister by six years. She has known you your entire life. She knew you as a toddler, as a teenager, as a young adult, as an adult, and as a parent and spouse. She knew you as a friend and a confidante. When you scraped your knees, got yelled at by your father, and had a fist fight with your best friend, she comforted you. She thinks she knows everything about you. In her heart, she believes you would not want to be kept on life support indefinitely. After much soul-searching, she knows you would want your family to let you go. Everything in your directives confirms what she believes.

The next day, she tells the doctors her decision.

Of your children, only Jet has any understanding that their aunt is involved in making such a decision. The twins are completely shielded. Jet knows more, but because the doctors, Teresa, Mitch, and your directives are all in agreement, he does not question the decision.

Teresa and Mitch arrange to have your bodies transported home so the joint funeral can take place in your town. Teresa and Mitch take your kids home with them. After the funeral, they send Jet back to college. They let your rental go, move the twins into their house, and put most of your belongings into storage until everyone can go through them together.

Teresa and Mitch are wonderful people; otherwise, you and Aiko would not have chosen them as your first-choice guardians. Yet they are not well off. Mitch drives a delivery truck for a local beverage company, and Teresa works for a florist. Their own children are grown, and they have settled into a smaller home. They have no money set aside for two extra mouths. They do everything in their power to raise the twins in accordance with your wishes, but taking on two teenagers is a colossal burden.

Olivia and Colin are both involved in numerous extracurricular activities, all of which cost money. They are going through growth spurts and more than double the household consumption of food, not to mention energy and water costs. Olivia wears glasses, and Colin needs braces.

Even more importantly, Olivia and Colin need more than just financial support. They have just lost both their parents and been moved into a new home. Many of their belongings and familiar surroundings are temporarily in storage. They feel disconnected from and alien to everything around them.

Teresa and Mitch would like to move into a bigger house so some of your belongings can be brought out of storage. At least then, Olivia and Colin can have some familiar surroundings. They would like the twins to have their own rooms and a used car. They would like to fund some family activities for the twins and Jet. They would like Teresa to give up her weekend shifts at the shop so she can spend more time with the twins.

Thank goodness you and Aiko splurged on a Personal Family Lawyer. Almost immediately after your death, Teresa and Mitch can access the money in the trust to meet your kids' needs, including grief counseling. The estate does not go through probate, a time-intensive and costly process that can freeze funds for twelve to eighteen months. And everything happens in the privacy of Ricardo's office as he guides Janice and Teresa with kindness and understanding throughout the whole process.

The money in the trust is administered and supervised by Janice, who simply ensures the money is used for its intended purpose: to care for your children. Teresa and Mitch do not need to petition the court for access to the money but need only submit requests to Janice. If it comes down to it and they can show Janice the twins need a full-time parent, Teresa will be able to obtain money from the trust so she can stay home until the twins turn eighteen. Once they do, the twins will be able to obtain funds directly from the trustee, as Jet already does. Janice shares your financial values, and she must approve all trust distributions until the kids turn thirty, at which point they will take over control of any remaining funds.

Your estate is not huge and will not last forever, but the money has been put into safe investments to earn a 5 percent or greater return. No one will get rich from your estate, but Teresa and Mitch are freed from the additional financial burden of your twins, and Jet can continue with college.

Additionally, your trust specifies the twins must go to college if they are to receive any additional access to trust assets once they turn eighteen. In this way, you have ensured that despite your and Aiko's modest assets, all three of your children will graduate from college. Your and Aiko's dream of starting a new tradition, in which all family members graduate from college, will be a reality despite your deaths.

With this guidance, Janice gives the same answer you would

when Olivia comes to her at nineteen and says, "I want to drop out of college and start a business instead. I need $25,000."

* * *

About six months after the accident, while Jet is on break, your family gets together to go through your personal belongings.

While your family is very close, each of your children is an individual with their own interests, quirks, and soft spots. Each inherited characteristics unique to you, and each inherited characteristics unique to Aiko. While you were alive, you loved seeing the melding that made you and Aiko such an unbreakable team.

Like Aiko, Jet loves animals. While the twins probably barely noticed them on the bookshelf, Jet loved the little menagerie of ceramic, glass, stone, wooden, and even plastic animals Aiko amassed. Other people might have eventually thrown away the silly wind-up plastic frog and duck, but Aiko never had been able to throw away an animal and added every silly one they found to the menagerie. The twins never commented on them, but Jet loved each of them since he was a baby, treasuring the additions as much as Aiko.

Olivia, on the other hand, loves books. She jealously guards every book she has ever been given. Even as a toddler, she pretended to read your old college textbooks. She always asks for books for gifts, and if other family members are not careful, she hoards their neglected books in her own room. If you ever thought about taking any of your old books to Goodwill, Olivia wanted them for herself. Her room is lined with bookshelves, and she swears she has read every one of them.

Colin loves photography. He uses his allowance to buy photography books, and he loves the framed photographs you and Aiko used to decorate your walls. None of the art is expensive, but Colin loves it all and wants to take pictures like that himself one day. He loves your Pentax LX, and when you were alive, he begged you to let him take pictures with it.

Because you thought about it ahead of time, you and Aiko specified, to the extent possible, who should receive all your personal belongings. Jet gets the first choice of anything animal related. Olivia gets first choice of any books, and Colin has dibs on photographic art and equipment. Your sister gets all your kitchenware. Mitch gets the tools and lawn equipment.

Although it is bittersweet, your family is able to bond a little over their experience at the storage facility. They open boxes together and then check your will (or separate writing outside your will) to see who is supposed to receive each item. They are able to share memories about you and Aiko related to your belongings. They remark upon particularly fitting designations. Some items are from your childhood and came to you through your parents. Teresa is able to share stories about your childhood with the kids, many of which they have never heard. Although several items are not designated for anyone, because each person thoughtfully has been given what mattered most, they are generous and honest with each other regarding the undesignated items. In the end, they all agree on boxes to be delivered to neighbors, other relatives, and local charities. They all feel a sense of catharsis from the day and closer as a family.

The last thing they do before going to bed that night is listen to the recording you made many, many years before, when you met with your Personal Family Lawyer to plan for your life and legacy. They hear you and Aiko talk about the life lessons you hoped to pass on and the love you felt for all of them. They will always feel the loss of their parents, but those feelings are lessened because they know you are always with them, which provides them with comfort and peace.

> Congratulations. Your choice to plan in advance for your life and legacy had the lasting impact of leaving your family in the best place possible after the tragedy of your deaths. Your children grow up to be incredible, strong, loving adults who contribute to making the world a better place.
>
> Turn to the Additional Resources at the end of the book for more resources on creating a lasting family legacy.

ADDITIONAL DISCLAIMERS

It is impossible to cover every situation that may occur in the event of your incapacity or when you die, which is why it's really important for you to meet with a Personal Family Lawyer to discuss your unique family dynamics and assets. However, there are two additional scenarios that bear mentioning here, though they don't appear in the choose-your-own-adventure format.

If you live internationally or are part of an unmarried domestic partnership, and especially if you are an unmarried parent, please read on for some considerations specific to you.

IF YOU LIVE INTERNATIONALLY

The three stories you just read all assume you live in the same country as your family of origin. If that's *not* the case for you, your planning just got exponentially more complicated—so much so that I couldn't even write a story that lets you choose your own adventure in any way that has a positive outcome without you working with a lawyer to ensure that if and when something happens to you while you are not in your home country, your family knows what to do and where to turn to take care of your affairs and ensure your children are not taken into the care of strangers.

Without taking the necessary precautions, you run the risk of your children being taken into the custody of your home country's embassy (if there is one) while authorities attempt to locate and notify your next of kin. There may be legal, financial, medical, and/or travel delays, which then compound delays for important decisions.

In this time of so many people living globally, your situation is complex enough that all I can advise you to do is to work with a lawyer to plan for the care of your children and your assets. And do it now.

Here's what to look for in a lawyer who can support you.

The right lawyer for you is not just going to have a short conversation with you and then prepare a set of documents. The right lawyer will have a procedure for getting to know you, your family dynamics, and your assets. They will guide you through an entire process of discovery to understand what you have, who you love, what your life is like now, and what you want it to be like in the future.

Then, they are going to educate you about the law based on the unique reality of where you live, where you travel, and how the law applies to your life and assets.

Only after that will they help you make decisions about what you need from a planning perspective to ensure you create the right documents with the right considerations for the people you love and your assets and that those documents remain up to date. They will not just create a will, trust, healthcare directive, and a power of attorney—although those documents will be part of a Life and Legacy Plan, they aren't the entirety of that plan.

The right lawyer for you is going to design a plan based on the specifics of your situation and your desires, which is going to use a combination of legal documents and other structures and strategies to ensure that if and when something happens to you, your family knows exactly what to do so there's no mess left behind—or if there is a mess, it's able to be cleaned up relatively easily.

IF YOU ARE PART OF AN UNMARRIED COUPLE, TRIAD, OR MORE

The risks you have read about in each of these stories apply exponentially if you are an unmarried parent—so read all of it again, but then consider that you do not have any of the built-in legal protections that marriage provides, such as having the built-in right to make legal and healthcare decisions for your partner.

When you are unmarried, if you have to be hospitalized and cannot make decisions for yourself, the law presumes your parents will make legal and healthcare decisions for you, and someone else would have to go to court to be appointed your guardian or agent to get access to your bank accounts in order to manage and pay your bills. If your parents aren't living, the law goes down the line to find your closest family member to make those decisions and manage your affairs for you.

This could mean your unmarried partner(s) would not have any say in your medical care and may not even be able to see you in the hospital. And your parents or siblings would decide who could see you in the hospital and how all healthcare decisions would be made on your behalf. If you are incapacitated for a long period or unexpectedly die, your unmarried partner(s) may even be forced to move out of a shared home in which they are not on a lease.

In your case, it is not wise to attempt your own legal planning, as there are simply too many variables at play. The good news is you can put in place even more intentional structures and systems for your care and the care of your children and assets, but you must do that with a lawyer who understands your unique needs; will get to know you, your family dynamics, your assets, and your desires; and will help you to craft the right plan for yourself and the people you love…a Life and Legacy Plan.

ADDITIONAL RESOURCES

FOR CHOOSING THE RIGHT GUARDIANS AND LEGALLY DOCUMENTING YOUR CHOICES

The guardian of your children is the person responsible for taking care of your children's physical, emotional, educational, and spiritual needs if you are unable to care for them. Approximately 69 percent of parents have not named legal guardians for their kids.[9] Of the 31 percent who have, most have made one of these common mistakes:

1. Naming a married couple to act as guardians and failing to provide instructions in case the named couple divorces or suffers the death of one spouse.
2. Not naming sufficient alternate guardians to serve if your first choice is unavailable.
3. Considering financial resources when deciding who should raise your children. Your guardians do not have to also be financial decision makers for your kids. They should be the people who will make the best healthcare, education, housing, discipline, and care decisions for your kids. It is your

---

9   Most statistics indicate that only about 30 percent of Americans have a will, and that has remained consistent for many years. Source: LegalZoom Staff, "Estate Planning Statistics," LegalZoom, last updated May 2, 2022, https://www.legalzoom.com/articles/estate-planning-statistics.

responsibility to leave enough money behind to take care of your kids, either through savings or life insurance; you can and should name someone other than the guardians of your children as guardians of the estate.

4. Not providing for someone to take care of the money you are leaving behind.

5. Naming only long-term care guardians and not making any arrangements for the immediate care of your children following your death or incapacity.

6. Not excluding anyone who might challenge your guardian decisions.

If you have minor children, regardless of the size of your bank account, you must legally document your decisions about who would raise them if you could not.

You can legally document your long-term guardian choices for free at KidsProtectionPlan.com plus have your legal nominations reviewed by a Personal Family Lawyer in your community at no charge. You will also find a simple, nine-step system for making sure your children will never be taken out of your home or raised by anyone you would not want serving as their guardian and the money you leave behind will be well taken care of by the right people.

Upon completing all nine steps, you can rest assured your children will be raised in accordance with your values, insights, stories, and experiences, growing into adults who would make you proud, are self-sufficient, and are satisfied with life.

WHEN AND WHERE YOU CAN CREATE OTHER LEGAL DOCUMENTS FOR FREE

Under certain circumstances—for example, if you are earlier in your adult life, don't have children, and/or have very few assets or straightforward estate planning needs—you may be able to create your legal documents for free or very inexpensively.

These documents can include a will, healthcare directive, and financial power of attorney.

- To create a will for free, visit lifelegacy.io or freewill.com.
- To create a healthcare directive, go to FiveWishes.org.
- To assign financial power of attorney, do an internet search for "durable power of attorney" in your state.

If you are unsure if these free services will keep your family out of court and conflict and serve to support you and your loved ones as you desire, please make an appointment to speak with a Personal Family Lawyer or go to PersonalFamilyLawyer.com to take our assessment on whether do-it-yourself planning can work for you or if you'll need legal support to keep your family out of court and from being stuck with a big mess.

FOR CHOOSING THE RIGHT TRUSTEES AND MAKING SMART FINANCIAL CHOICES

As parents, we have a myriad of financial decisions to make for our children—decisions that impact not only their futures but future generations as well.

It is your responsibility as a parent to leave behind sufficient financial resources for whoever will be caring for your child if you cannot. You can do this through savings or life insurance. For guidance on what kind of and how much life insurance is right for your family, see our articles on PersonalFamilyLawyer.com.

The best way to make sure your financial resources will be immediately available to your children or their guardian is to leave behind an up-to-date Life and Legacy Plan with a trusted lawyer to guide the people you've chosen to take care of your children and assets.

WHETHER YOU HAVE A LOT OR A LITTLE, DON'T LOSE IT

Regardless of the size of your assets, you want to make sure your financial resources will be available immediately to your children and/or their guardian if something happens to you and that the people you've chosen to care for your children know what you have, where to find it, and how to get access to it.

The biggest risk to the people you love, whether you have existing estate planning documents or not, is that they will not know what you have or how to find it.

So, we've created a solution to make sure that at the very least what you have is inventoried so you can leave behind a treasure map of sorts for the people you love.

You can access the free Personal Resource Map tool plus watch a training video with me to clarify what you can do yourself and what you need a lawyer to handle with you at PersonalResourceMap.com.

ACKNOWLEDGMENTS

First and foremost, none of this would have ever been known or created without my children, Kaia and Noah. Now that you are adults, we get to put in place your Life and Legacy Plans. How amazing and wonderful is that? And, of course, papa Todd Neely. We may have divorced in 2005, but your continued presence in our life has made so much possible. I love you and thank you.

Next, deep gratitude to the folks at Scribe and especially to Jenny Shipley for the expert editing and collaboration on this Second Edition.

Finally, to the New Law Business Model team and every Personal Family Lawyer I love. I never imagined I could love lawyers so much or that I would love being a lawyer so much—and it's all because of you. Thank you for your yes to becoming the expert legal educators in your communities and for serving your clients as you do. You are what has me keep on keeping on, even when I want to give it all up and move back to the farm.

ABOUT THE AUTHOR

 **ALI KATZ** (prior legal name: Alexis Martin Neely, CA Bar: 212365) is a nationally recognized authority, author, and speaker on family, financial, and legal matters. After graduating first in her class from Georgetown Law, she was recognized by *Worth* early on in her law career as one of the country's top-100 lawyers. She began her work as an associate lawyer at the firm of Munger, Tolls & Olson and then went on to establish her own law firm, Martin Neely & Associates, as well as New Law Business Model, a training company for new paradigm law, and the Family Wealth Planning Institute, a nationwide collective of Personal Family Lawyer firms trained and licensed to use Ali's heart-centered counseling-based methodology to serve their clients.

Ali is the creator of KidsProtectonPlan.com, a website that guides parents through a three-step process to help them decide who should be named guardians for their kids, teaches them the six common mistakes many parents make, and allows them to legally document their choices, all absolutely free.

Most importantly, Ali is driven by her vision of preparing her own kids, Kaia and Noah, for lives of wealth, health, and happiness.

Ingram Content Group UK Ltd.
Milton Keynes UK
UKHW011821160323
418676UK00001B/80

9 781544 535883